HOW TO ACT LIKE A KID

HOW TO ACT LIKE A KID

Backstage Secrets of a Young Performer

HENRY HODGES & MARGARET ENGEL

EDITIONS

New York

For information address Disney Editions,
114 Fifth Avenue, New York, New York 10011-5690.

Mary Poppins is based on the Walt Disney motion picture
Mary Poppins, based on the series of books by P. L. Travers.
The Little Mermaid © Disney Enterprises, Inc.

ISBN 978-1-4231-6320-6
V381-8386-5-13091

First Edition
10 9 8 7 6 5 4 3 2 1
Printed in the United States of America

The Official Disney Fan Club

Disney.com/D23

Visit www.disneybooks.com

This book is dedicated
to my family
for their never-ending support and encouragement;
to Tom Schumacher,
who asked the question, "What is it like to be a child performer?";
to Ridley Pearson,
who listened to my answer;
and to Wendy Lefkon,
who believed that I could develop that answer into this book.

—H.H.

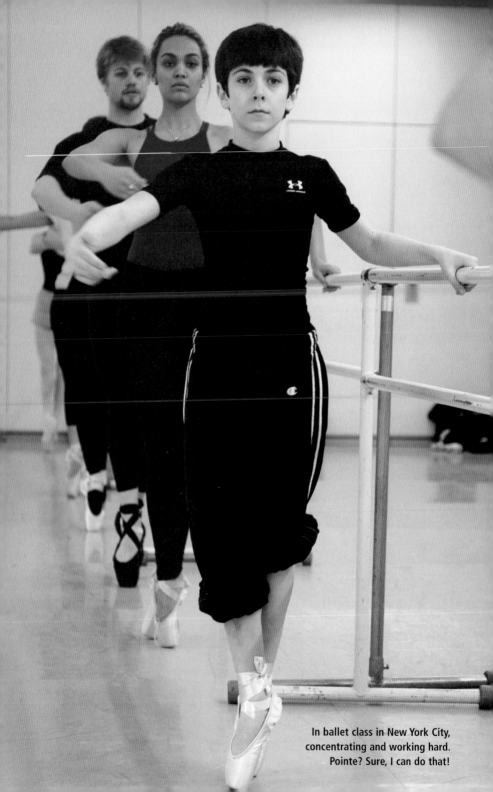

In ballet class in New York City,
concentrating and working hard.
Pointe? Sure, I can do that!

Contents

Foreword

Thomas Schumacher
with Henry Hodges and Margaret Engel

Tom Schumacher, president of Disney Theatrical Group, sat down in his office at the New Amsterdam Theatre in New York City in November 2012 with the authors to talk about acting as a kid—and as an adult.

Tom Schumacher: Henry is the best thing you can have in a child performer, because he is an old soul. With Henry, even though you're seeing an actor who is apparently a child and represents himself to the audience as a child, you have someone who has extraordinary intellect, great emotional depth, and the ability to function within a production. Add to that Henry's extraordinary physical acuity—the waveboard, in addition to the unicycle—there's always a new gadget. It's gigantically helpful to have a kid like Henry.

Margaret Engel: Is it scary to have your fortunes riding on such small shoulders?

TS: When an audience comes to a show and there's a range of characters from kids to adults, it changes the tone backstage, it changes the performance—it gives every level of the audience some entry point. When kids are watching Henry play Michael Banks in *Mary Poppins*, they're seeing the show through his eyes. That's their entry point.

ME: What is it like, Henry, to be that one who gets to be that special kid onstage?

TS: Do you think about that?

HH: Yeah, I obsess over it. Towards the end of auditioning for *Mary Poppins*, I was aware I had a decent chance of getting it.

TS: Didn't you think you were just going to nail it? Just get it right away? With your dad being British, and what you looked like?

With Tom at his favorite table at Sardi's, the famous New York Theater District restaurant where you feel as if all of Broadway history is staring down at you. I was in *Mary Poppins* on Broadway at the time.

HH: No. Remember the first auditions, the kids were kind of small. I was one of the tallest kids there. And then the girls started to get slightly bigger and that really gave me hope. By the last audition, I was fairly certain.

ME: Why have you devoted your career to entertainment based on children's stories?

TS: We don't just do children's theater. People think it's family entertainment. But what's family? It's grandpa and grandma and the kids and the crazy uncle and the goofy sister. Families are not safe, easy things. They're complex. They're difficult. They're challenging. And they're loving. If we can get all that into a show! Henry was horribly bratty at the top of *Mary Poppins*. He was a rotten, rotten little kid. But at the end when he says, "I love you, Mary Poppins," the whole audience falls apart.

HH: During the rehearsals the character's journey became more apparent to me, how that could be accomplished.

TS: You know how crazy I was about Henry's performance. He was just so great in the show, and I just loved everything he did. But Henry's height

I love visiting Tom's office, which is filled with drawings and memorabilia from shows he has produced. Two of my favorite items are the scale model *Mary Poppins* set behind Tom and the clown shoe on the bookshelf. We are looking over sample layouts for Tom's book *How Does the Show Go On?*

became a problem. It's not like he's going to play professional basketball at this point. But still he got too big to play the part. There was this giant person on the stage.

HH: And I was supposed to be an eight-year-old.

TS: He was just too big. So I said, "Don't worry, I'll tell him. I'll break this shocking news." This is one of my favorite memories of Henry, which speaks to the old-soul thing—remember this? And so we had this meeting in the dressing room. We're chatting, and I had this whole windup, and I take my time, and I'm preparing for this huge emotional outburst, and he says, "Okay." It was a totally non-emotional response. He totally got it. *Okay, I'm too big for it. Next?*

ME: At that point, you were what age?

HH: I was just about fifteen.

TS: Going on forty.

ME: How can child stars stay grounded?

TS: Obviously, parents play a huge part in creating the nightmare child as well as the successful child. Child actors have to want to be doing this. They shouldn't be doing it to please someone else. This has to be their bliss. To be trained and have skill and talent is hugely important. Kids can be naturals. But they are like athletes in the same way that kids prepare for gymnastics in the Olympics. They start at seven years old. Does anyone know what they want later? No. That's why so many kids have had Henry's experience and then they go on to other things. That's reasonable.

ME: How do successful child performers like Henry who want to keep working transition to a career as an adult?

TS: They get the right roles. For me, with Henry, the real transformative moment was to see him in *To Kill a Mockingbird*, because he was just so beautiful onstage and had such depth. I took a very long drive to see him in a matinee at Hartford Stage. It was so beautiful. And then the Horton Foote play Henry was in, *The Orphans' Home Cycle*—that was a weep-fest for me. A complete weep-fest. He was a kid, but now he's an adult. Isn't that a shocking thing?

Letter to Readers

Dear Reader,

You may be the understudy for the lead in your high school musical. You may have rocked the villain's part at drama camp last summer. In your living room right now, you may be rehearsing your future star turn on *American Idol*.

Whatever your dreams, we think putting yourself onstage is a worthy endeavor. Learning to communicate clearly and move with confidence, and the discipline instilled by learning to dance, sing, and play music, give you lifelong skills that cannot be taken from you, no matter what the outcome of auditions may be.

We wrote this book because its subject, Henry Hodges, started out as a true rookie, but he has made it to Broadway in multiple blockbuster shows, including *Mary Poppins*, *Chitty Chitty Bang Bang*, and *Beauty and the Beast*. He didn't have friends or relatives in show business. He lives in Bethesda, Maryland, quite a distance from the Great White Way.

He and his family learned a lot as he grew from a five-year-old in a Mattel toy commercial to a teenager signing autographs for screaming fans outside the New Amsterdam Theatre on Forty-Second Street in New York City. From community theater to opera to touring shows, voice-overs, and stage dramas, Henry has practical advice to offer you on the training and attitude you need to make it in the highly competitive world of performance.

Henry hopes you will be interested in how he prepares himself for work on the stage, radio, commercials, television, and movies. And we believe his story can help thousands of aspiring young actors adopt the work habits and down-to-earth perspective that have made his successful climb happy, educational, and fulfilling.

The performing arts can be a great foundation for success as an adult. We hope you enjoy Henry's journey and that it will help you delight in your own travels into the spotlight.

Sincerely,

Margaret Engel

HI! I'm Henry!

A Few Words from Henry

It's fair to say that becoming a performer saved my life. I'm not being melodramatic. My years in elementary school were awful.

Even though I repeated kindergarten and was the oldest in my class, I was always the smallest kid in the class. There's something funny about being turned down—two years in a row—for the role of Tiny Tim in *A Christmas Carol* because you're *too tiny*.

I was so small that doctors kept trying to convince my parents to give me shots of growth hormones so I'd be "normal." Luckily, my parents never agreed.

I have serious dyslexia, which meant I couldn't read in elementary school. I spent my time in school pretending or getting stomachaches. Every chance I could, I'd escape to the nurse's office.

I liked going on the bus, eating in the cafeteria, and physical education. But in class, I'd be frantically saying to myself, *Don't call on me, don't call on me!*

I couldn't spell. I wasn't even good in art. I always felt so ashamed. I couldn't get it and I didn't know why. I felt like such an idiot because I didn't know anything.

I figured out how to skip class for three months while I was still going to school. I was in a special-needs class for reading and I would simply tell one teacher I was in the other class. I would just roam the hallways and walk up and down the stairwells.

My teacher told me she was giving one of my writing assignments an F because there weren't enough periods in it. I remember going into the bathroom and adding a period after every word. *I'll give you tons of periods!* I decided. The teacher said I was being a smart aleck.

In the rest of my world, I was used to succeeding. Life with my older sister, Charly, our parents, and our dog, Pucci, was a blast. It was school that made me feel terrible.

Here's what turned things around for me: failure.

I was getting a "not passing" grade in music. I was seven years old.

My mom asked why. "He can't sing the songs," the teacher said. "He can't follow the bouncing ball above the words on the screen."

My mom pulled me out of music class and got the school's permission to substitute private lessons at the Levine School of Music, which was nearby. That was the beginning of my starting to learn to sing. I learned to breathe right and got introduced to vibrato, vocalizing, and scales. Since I was so young, I didn't have any major bad habits. My mom would tape the classes and we'd go over them at home.

This was the start of my theater career. We started seeing notices of auditions on bulletin boards at the school, and my mom started talking with other moms whose kids sang or acted in local productions.

My two big negatives—my size and my dyslexia—helped launch me into a world where I succeeded beyond what I could have imagined.

As a young actor, my dyslexia affected my ability to read, write, and spell. While I was performing in *Mary Poppins*, my tutor, Muriel Kester, learned that ventriloquist Jay Johnson, who was also appearing on Broadway at the time, is dyslexic too, and suggested that I write to him. Here is the letter I sent Jay. Jay is a really open and fun-filled guy. When we met, he taught me how to make origami good-luck cranes out of dollar bills.

Dear Mr. Johnson   1/24/06

I am 13 and I am plaing Michael in Mary Poppins on Brodway in the NEW Amsterdam. My tutur saw you on TV and told me about you. We have a lot in commen. I am an actor. I was in chitty chitty BangBang and Butty and the Best. I am dyslexic, just like you. I admier your werk and would like to met you to find out how you overcame your dyslexia wen you were a child. I wud love to mete you or talk to you. My Cell is 301-████. And I am sending you m' pichter and bio frum our show Bill. Plees call me our e-mail me at ████@AOL.com

Sinserlly
Henry Hodges

P.S. No one in the show nos I am dyslexic exept the Kids. Pllees Keep this a scret. Thanks.

HENRY HODGES (Michael Banks at certain performances). Broadway: originated the role of Jeremy Potts in *Chitty Chitty Bang Bang*. Broadway and national tour: *Beauty and the Beast* (Chip). Regional: Ford's Theatre. *A Christmas Carol* (Tiny Tim); Kirov Opera's *Macbeth*; Washington Opera's *Madama Butterfly*, *Salome* and *Idomeneo* with Placido Domingo. Also, *The Yellow Dress* ballet at Lincoln Center. Numerous recordings, commercials, voiceovers, films. TV includes HBO, PBS-Satellite. www.HenryHodges.com

1

The Thrill of Getting to Perform on Broadway

It's an amazing kick to see a huge billboard for your show in Times Square!

I stood in New York's busy Times Square, staring up at its famous JumboTron. There I was singing on its huge screen, as a twelve-year-old, with thousands of people watching. That was a thrill, and was just one of many unexpected perks that being a performer has brought me.

First, there are the fun theater traditions I learned. On opening night, it is customary to give presents to everyone in the hours before the curtain rises. You plan for days on what to give and you put fun, meaningful gifts in dressing rooms and crew offices. It looked like Christmas in my dressing room before some shows!

For *Mary Poppins*, I was given a plate from Tiffany jewelers from the president of Disney Theatrical Productions, with the image of the front of the house on Cherry Tree Lane and the date of opening night engraved on it. Other presents were a handmade bowler hat made to fit my head, the original *Mary Poppins* music handwritten and signed by its composers, and an electric scooter that Alma Cuervo, who played the part of Mrs. Potts, my character's mom in *Beauty and the Beast*, carried seven flights of stairs up to my dressing room.

For *Chitty Chitty Bang Bang*, I wrote a long letter to everyone in the show, thanking them all for their friendship and making a donation in their name to a charity. For other shows, my mom and I baked cookies

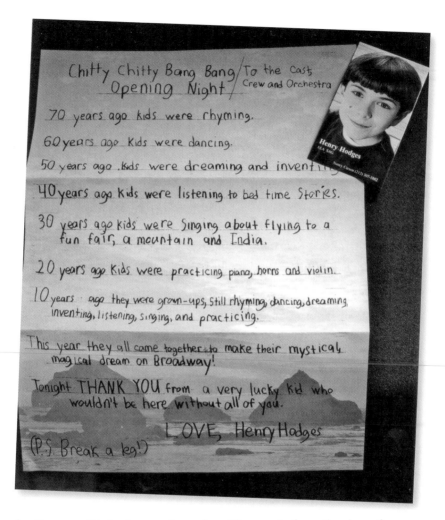

Chitty Chitty Bang Bang/To the Cast,
Opening Night/ Crew and Orchestra

70 years ago kids were rhyming.

60 years ago kids were dancing.

50 years ago kids were dreaming and inventi

40 years ago kids were listening to bed time stories.

30 years ago kids were singing about flying to a
fun fair, a mountain and India.

20 years ago kids were practicing piano, horns and violin.

10 years ago they were grown-ups, still rhyming, dancing, dreaming,
inventing, listening, singing, and practicing.

This year they all came together to make their mystical,
magical dream on Broadway!

Tonight THANK YOU from a very lucky kid who
wouldn't be here without all of you.

LOVE, Henry Hodges

(P.S. Break a leg!)

for the crew. We had magnets made, with a quote from the show, for
Macbeth and *To Kill a Mockingbird*.

Another custom I learned was the gypsy robe ceremony for Broadway
musicals. This event is held just before the curtain goes up before opening
night. The show is given a robe from Actors' Equity that has the logos and
designs from other musicals that have opened recently.

The "gypsy" in the cast, which is the ensemble member (singer, dancer,
or nonprincipal actor who moves from show to show) who has been in

Parts I Have Played

Here are some of my favorite roles—and some of my favorite costumes!

- The youngest prince of Siam in *The King and I*, with The Arlington Players in suburban Virginia—my first theatrical show

- Tiny Tim, a five-year-old London boy, in *A Christmas Carol*, at Ford's Theatre in Washington, DC

Here I am with my "mom" as the youngest prince of Siam in my first theatrical show, *The King and I*, with The Arlington Players in suburban Virginia. I was 8 years old.

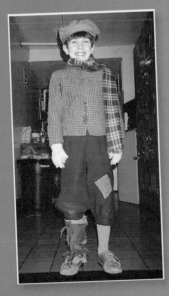

Finally, I get to play Tiny Tim. I performed this role two years in a row, starting when I was 8 years old.

- Neptune's Sacrifice, in the Kennedy Center production of Mozart's opera *Idomeneo*, in which the title character was sung by Placido Domingo

- Chip, Mrs. Potts's eight-year-old teacup son in *Beauty and the Beast*, on Broadway and in the national tour

- Jeremy Potts, an eight-year-old British boy, in *Chitty Chitty Bang Bang* on Broadway

- Michael Banks, a nine-year-old London boy, in the Broadway production of *Mary Poppins*

I got to wear a foam teacup on my head as Chip. Most of my time was spent with just my head popping out of a box. This is why I wore all-black clothes ("blacks") for the rest of my costume. It was a great exercise at age 9 to learn how to express my emotions using only my face. During all the dance numbers, I "danced" along with my head, making specific movements the show choreographers called "cupography."

- Mudbud, the "surfer dude" golden retriever puppy, in the Disney films *Snow Buddies* and *Space Buddies*, as the role's "voice actor"

- Fleance, son of Banquo, and Macduff's son in William Shakespeare's *Macbeth* on Broadway

- Jem, a twelve-year-old Alabama boy, in *To Kill a Mockingbird*, at Hartford Stage in Connecticut

- Horace Robedaux, a fourteen-year-old Southern youth, in *The Orphans' Home Cycle*, both Off Broadway and at Hartford Stage

- Flounder, Ariel's sixteen-year-old best fish friend in the European touring version of *The Little Mermaid*

On Broadway, the character of Flounder in *The Little Mermaid* was a small boy. In the reimagined European version, Flounder is 16. What a fun costume! Many of the costumes in this production were the Broadway originals, but this one was made to fit me by the amazing costumers at the Sacramento Music Circus.

There are so many great gypsy robes, it's hard to choose just one! Here, Carlos L. Encinias, an actor in *Scandalous: The Life and Trials of Aimee Semple McPherson*, models a new robe during the Broadway Opening Night Gypsy Robe Ceremony at the Al Hirschfeld Theatre in 2012, celebrating Timothy J. Alex's performance in the musical *Elf*.

the most Broadway shows, is presented with the robe onstage, about an hour before the curtain. This is a serious ceremony, with everyone holding hands in a circle while the stage lights are low, praying for luck on the show. The gypsy puts on the robe and runs counterclockwise around the circle three times, touching everyone's hands for luck. The gypsy then goes from dressing room to dressing room, and the actors touch the robe for luck.

Later, the show's costume designers, using fabric from the actual costumes and memorabilia from the show, decorate a panel on the robe. All the cast and crew members sign the panel too. The robe is stored in the costume room until the gypsy takes it to the next musical's opening night to award it to another gypsy.

Casts have been doing this since 1950 when a chorus member of *Gentlemen Prefer Blondes* gave a dressing gown to the cast of *Call Me Madam*, saying the Ziegfeld dancers had worn the robe and would "bless" the new show. That's how the tradition started.

A robe is filled up after about a dozen musicals have added their decorations. Many of the robes from the early years have been lost, but Actors' Equity Association now keeps the robes. One is always on display at the Actors' Equity Audition Center in New York City.

The ceremony helped me understand how much is riding on a Broadway show's success—so many jobs and livelihoods are at risk. It's also a very special event that's closed to outsiders and helps make the theater family tight knit and one of a kind.

We kids in *Chitty Chitty Bang Bang* helped raise money for the Gypsy of the Year benefit that Broadway Cares/Equity Fights AIDS arranges. Our child wrangler, Vanessa Brown, wrote a skit we performed, and we won second place (after *Lion King*, which always wins because of its great dancers).

There's also the tradition of all the cast members signing a hand-painted poster of a touring show on a backstage wall of many theaters. Whoever is most talented artistically in a show—and there is always a very good artist—draws the poster, and then everyone signs his or her name. A run of a show is so temporary that it's nice to see all of the famous and not-so-famous people who came before you memorialized on a wall of a theater where you are working. Everyone makes their mark! I had a lot of fun in the twenty-one cities where we toured for *Beauty and the Beast*, from Pittsburgh to Indianapolis to St. Louis, signing my name on the walls.

It's also a thrill getting to sign autographs at the stage door after a show. Sometimes kids in the crowd will even scream once you come out the door! If it's raining, the stage-door security guards will hold umbrellas for you.

When I was really young, people didn't know that *all* I could sign was my name. If they asked me, "Write 'To Aunt Carrie,' please," I couldn't! During the *Beauty and the Beast* tour, young girls seeing the show would

Steven Reeves, the stage-door security guard for *Mary Poppins*, who was super nice, holds an umbrella over us as star Ashley Brown (Mary Poppins) and I sign autographs in the rain.

come dressed up as Belle. I got my picture taken many times with young Belles of all ages. I always stay after to sign autographs, because I am so grateful that people come to our shows and like them. Fans are awesome.

One of the nicest things that continually happens is that moms and teachers who don't know me routinely come up after the show to say they are proud of me. Isn't that amazing?

Since I work on Broadway, there are some New York–only events I get to do. How about getting to sing and dance in the Macy's Thanksgiving Day Parade? Or singing in Shubert Alley for the annual Stars in the Alley end-of-season free show organized by the Broadway League? There, I got to sing "Truly Scrumptious" with Erin Dilly, the female lead of *Chitty Chitty Bang Bang*, on a stage built in the alley. Thousands of Broadway fans come to this event to see their favorite stars up close.

Because *Mary Poppins* was nominated for several Tony Awards, I got to join the cast one year to sing onstage at Radio City Music Hall (a gigantic theater with 5,931 seats) for the Tony Awards ceremony, which airs

With one of my *Mary Poppins* "sisters," Kathryn Faughnan, waving to the audience after performing "Supercal" at Broadway on Broadway. Of all the young actresses I worked with in this show, Kathryn was the most like my real sister, Charly. Kathryn looks a bit like Charly, and she makes me laugh, just as Charly does.

nationwide annually on network TV. When I was part of the *Chitty Chitty Bang Bang* cast, we performed on the *Today* show and the Jerry Lewis Muscular Dystrophy Labor Day Telethon.

For Kids' Night on Broadway, I emceed an event with actor Corbin Bleu at Madame Tussauds New York wax museum. That was a blast. For Broadway on Broadway, a free outdoor concert that kicks off the theater season each September, I got to climb up on another temporary stage built in Times Square and sing "Supercal" (you know the rest of the title!) from *Mary Poppins*. The performers from dozens of musicals take the stage for that fun event.

One of my biggest thrills was getting to introduce my friend Tom Schumacher, the president of Disney Theatrical Productions, when his caricature was put up in Sardi's, the famous theater restaurant. Caricatures of stars and theater people line the walls of Sardi's, which has been an industry hangout for ninety years on West Forty-Fourth Street. Many opening-night parties are held there, as it's surrounded by theaters.

You look forward to the opening and closing parties to make up for all the hard work in rehearsals and onstage. On the opening night of *Chitty Chitty Bang Bang*, I got to meet the original Jeremy (Adrian Hall) and Jemima Potts (Heather Ripley) from the 1968 movie. They flew in from the United Kingdom for the event. They understood what a fun experience it was for me to be in the same show they starred in.

Without a doubt, that opening night celebration for *Chitty Chitty Bang Bang* was the most extravagant party I have ever attended on Broadway. The party took the show's "fun fair" and "sweets factory" scenes and ran with them. There were clowns, stilt walkers, and magicians. I have never seen so much candy in my life. There was a huge table in the middle with a many-tiered fountain filled with liquid chocolate, surrounded by a toy train carrying all kinds of sweets around on train tracks. All the kids ate candy all night.

I especially liked the little white paper containers filled with red Jell-O. We all grabbed the containers from the train as it raced around. It wasn't until a few days later that I found out those Jell-O cups were Jell-O *shots*—Jell-O mixed with vodka! Whose idea was it to put Jell-O shots on a toy train going around a table filled with candy? I guess they thought our parents or child wranglers would be investigating this candy buffet. Luckily, no one suffered any ill effects.

Ellen Marlow, who played the part of my twin sister, and I pose with the actors who played our characters in the 1968 film *Chitty Chitty Bang Bang*. Adrian Hall (Jeremy) and Heather Ripley (Jemima) flew in from London to see the opening night of the show on Broadway. We got really dressed up for the opening night party at the Hilton hotel in New York City. I wore my cowboy boots to make me taller!

For the thirteenth anniversary of *Beauty and the Beast* at the Lunt-Fontanne Theatre in New York, there was a reunion of 250 of the former cast members. This included several dozen of the boys who had played Chip over the years. We all assembled by the castle onstage for a group photo.

Being in *Mary Poppins* allowed me to meet and be photographed with the mayor of New York City, Michael Bloomberg. He held a barbecue dinner at Gracie Mansion to thank the cast and crew for helping him produce a spoof show, *Mayor Poppins*, in which Mayor Bloomberg played the lead role and I played the young Mayor Bloomberg. The spoof was presented to a hundred members of the New York City press corps at an annual event to raise money for city charities.

Nearly all of the Broadway shows field softball teams in the spring that

I'm in the middle here, at a reunion of some of the actors who had played Chip in *Beauty and the Beast*, in front of the castle at the Lunt-Fontanne Theatre in New York. There were more than 250 cast members at the party. I asked one of the former Chips what he'd been up to recently and he said he was married and had two kids!

play in Central Park on Thursday mornings. Many of the shows bring cloth banners, sewn by the costume staffs, to cheer their teams on. I played on the *Beauty and the Beast* team until someone discovered that you have to be sixteen to play. I was only eleven, so I was switched to batboy. At least my team won second place.

Keeping score for the *Beauty and the Beast* softball team's regular weekly game in Central Park. I played a few innings in one game—and I even scored a run!—until a worried-looking woman ran out onto the field and asked if I was 16! Benched! (But my run still counted.) After that, I had to be batboy or score keeper. We won second place for the season, behind the team from *The Producers*. I also got to keep the uniform, which I will grow into any day now. . . .

What I Do Backstage in the Greenroom

The greenroom is a room in every theater where actors can rest during stage rehearsals and performances when they are not needed onstage but don't want to go all the way back to their dressing room. Here are some of my favorite backstage pastimes.

- Finish my homework

- Watch movies

- Play video games

- Work on model kits (snap-together kits—no glue that might damage your costume!)

- Assemble jigsaw puzzles

There were other surprises on Broadway. In big-budget shows, your dressing gown is embroidered with your name. That's cool! There are also "Happy Trails" parties when a cast member leaves the show, when everyone takes lots of photos. Another fun moment was when my friend the late Bob Sherman, the coauthor of the *Mary Poppins* music, had the famous Carnegie Deli put my headshot on the wall. Ashley Brown, who played Mary Poppins, went to the deli for a bagel the next morning. She pointed out to the whole cast, laughing, that she didn't have that honor, but I did!

As an audience member, I never knew about the customary backstage activities, like the cast and crew having birthday parties during intermissions. That happens about twice a month in a show with a large cast. If there are animals in a show, they are kept in kennels backstage that meet the Humane Society's rules. During *Chitty Chitty Bang Bang*, we kid actors got to visit the eight dogs that were part of the show during intermissions and before the show.

The backstage crew members have interesting jobs. Since science is my favorite school subject and I am fascinated by how things work, I spent time with the guys who prep props and handle equipment. They let me try on welding helmets, learn about lights, and understand how the whole ballet of the backstage works.

There also can be great kindness backstage. Kimberly Breault, part of the *Beauty and the Beast* ensemble, knew I had dyslexia. She read many

Kimberly Breault, a *Beauty and the Beast* ensemble member, read to me backstage during our national tour after she found out I had dyslexia. She picked out the books and gave them to me when the tour ended. My favorite was *The Lion, the Witch and the Wardrobe*.

My dream of becoming the Phantom of the Opera came true, thanks to Vincent Schicchi, the prosthetics specialist for *Beauty and the Beast.* Here he is (*left*) putting a foam rubber prosthetics on my face. It took him about 90 minutes. And here I am (*right*), ready to take on Halloween as the Phantom. I'm in the Chip dressing room. The room was filled with artwork by former Chips. At left is a picture in crayon of a chocolate "Chip" cookie. *Ha-ha*—get it?

books to me backstage, including my favorites, *A Wrinkle in Time* and *The Lion, the Witch and the Wardrobe.*

When I was eleven, I got special Halloween makeup created by Vincent Schicchi, the prosthetics specialist for *Beauty and the Beast.* Vinny did the four hours of makeup for the Beast every night and has worked on many films such as *Men in Black 3* and *The Amazing Spider-Man.*

Because he's a nice guy, he spent ninety minutes working with rubber foam to make me look like the real Phantom of the Opera. I was the hit of the party at our apartment building, wearing a black cape and huge

Some of the Stars I Have Met

I feel so fortunate to have met some of the great stars who have inspired me as a performer—and to have worked with some of them too.

- Denzel Washington and Yoko Ono, while rehearsing in studios on Forty-Second Street in New York

- Hugh Jackman, who was appearing in *The Boy from Oz* in a Broadway theater across the street when I was in *Beauty and the Beast*

- Jane Fonda, at the Drama Desk Awards party

Jane Fonda brought her dog, Tulea, to the Drama Desk Awards in New York City.

Signing autographs with Hugh Jackman outside in the cold.

When Donny Osmond appeared in *Beauty and the Beast*, he found time to record an entire album in his dressing room during downtime!

Singing with
Rosie O'Donnell.

With Broadway
veteran Angela Lansbury at the
Drama Desk Awards.

- Angela Lansbury, at a gala to raise funds for the Signature Theatre in New York

- Rosie O'Donnell, singing an impromptu duet of "I've Got You Two" from *Chitty Chitty Bang Bang* with me at a launch party for my friend Euan Morton's CD at Joe's Pub in New York City

With Placido Domingo in my first opera, *Idomeneo*, at the Kennedy Center.

Cynthia Nixon, one of the four stars of *Sex and the City*, came backstage after seeing *Mary Poppins*.

I was part of the cast that performed a spoof, *Mayor Poppins*, for New York Mayor Michael Bloomberg and the press corps at Gracie Mansion.

Continues . . .

Some of the Stars I Have Met *(continued)*

- Composer Alan Menken, who autographed one of Gaston's beer steins for me after seeing *Beauty and the Beast*, for which Menken wrote the music, while we were on tour

- Jonathan Groff, of *Spring Awakening* and *Glee*

- Beau Bridges and T. R. Knight (of *Grey's Anatomy*), both of whom I met doing readings

- Sandra Bullock, with whom I read lines for four days on a film project in New York City

With Alan Menken, holding the mug he signed for me.

With Beau Bridges; we had just participated in a reading of the script that became *A Christmas Story: The Musical* on Broadway.

With Jonathan Groff at Birdland in New York; Jonathan had just sung in the Leading Man IV concert.

Appearing with Patrick Stewart in *Macbeth* on Broadway was exciting.

With Corbin Bleu at Kids' Night on Broadway.

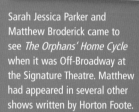

Sarah Jessica Parker and Matthew Broderick came to see *The Orphans' Home Cycle* when it was Off-Broadway at the Signature Theatre. Matthew had appeared in several other shows written by Horton Foote.

Eating cake with Matthew Modine at the closing party for *To Kill a Mockingbird*.

collar. Vinny also created a *Dawn of the Dead* sculpted version of my character, Chip, for me as a present, with his jaw ripped off and an eye hanging down. I have it hanging on my bedroom wall with my show posters.

Having the whole city of New York to play in on your days off is special too. I learned to ride a unicycle holding the long railing along the Hudson River in front of where the USS *Intrepid* is docked. I get to skimboard at Brooklyn's Brighton Beach. Because many top magicians call New York home, there are great magic shops here. I've learned a lot of tricks from hanging around the Fantasma Magic shop on Seventh Avenue.

"Chip of the Living Dead"
For Henry—
My favorite "Chip"
Hope you like it . . .
Your Friend
Vinny

Here's where I learned to steady myself on a unicycle—using the railing along the Hudson River, next to the USS *Intrepid*. I decided to learn how to ride a unicycle at age 15 when I saw one in the window of a bike shop in New York's Hell's Kitchen neighborhood.

Can you believe this beach is just a subway ride away from New York City? I love whipping out to Brighton Beach on my day off and hangin' in the surf on my skimboard.

As a working actor, of course I get to meet the stars in my own shows. But I pretty regularly meet other famous actors at cast parties and table readings. (You can be hired just to read scripts around a table, for musicals, straight plays, or films in their early stages.) It has been exciting to meet many of these huge talents. Getting to act with Patrick Stewart in *Macbeth* on Broadway was unreal at first. He was so nice and fun to work with, even if he can terrify an audience when he's in character. When I was appearing in four operas at the Kennedy Center (in Washington, DC), where Placido Domingo was the music director, I remember the nightly announcement over the dressing room loudspeaker before our scene together: "Will Mr. Domingo and Mr. Hodges please meet at the elevator." Now that doesn't happen to your typical nine-year-old.

You don't go into the performing arts with a goal of winning prizes, but they are nice perks when they happen. The cast of *The Orphans' Home Cycle*, including me, won a Drama Desk Award, an Outer Critics Circle Award, and a New York Drama Critics' Circle Award. Those award ceremonies and parties were fun, and I met Jane Fonda, and her dog, Tulea, at one of them.

Another bonus of so-called fame is having the press write about you. My picture has been on websites such as BroadwayWorld.com and Playbill. com, and stories have been written in local and national magazines and newspapers on me. It never gets old seeing your face on billboards and posters either.

With Nicole Bocchi, who played Jane Banks in *Mary Poppins*, flying a Poppins kite by the Hudson River in New York.

2

Teachers and Coaches

Everyone got a carnation from the teacher at the recital for the beginning boy's class at the Maryland Youth Ballet. I was 8 years old here. So few boys took ballet that for a while, I got free lessons.

Like thousands of other toddlers, I was considered a cute kid. I started modeling clothes for Wrangler in a magazine ad when I was five, after my mom's doctor—whose mother had been an agent for young performers—suggested that I would be good for that kind of work.

Getting Started: Parents, Coaches, and Instructors

My career started when I was four and my mom saw a notice posted on a school bulletin board by a local child manager inviting parents to an information session. My mom attended, and a few days later I was among a hundred kids at an audition in a classroom with a small raised stage. I sang my ABCs for the manager. When you're very young, all you sing for auditions are the ABCs or "Happy Birthday."

We waited an hour while the manager interviewed the other kids, and then she told us she wanted to represent me. She mailed us a list of

photographers to consider for headshots. Then we waited for her to call us for auditions, most of them for commercials. My mom had to be ready to take me to Baltimore, to Philadelphia, to

I was 7 years old in this shoot for an InterContinental Hotels ad photographed in the chain's Washington, DC, hotel. The art directors folded the clothes in the top drawer and I spent the entire day pulling everything out and throwing it up in the air. I also ran down the hall in a blue bathrobe over and over again. I must have been easily entertained because I remember thinking how much fun it was. Afterward, they gave me all the brand-new clothes to keep. It was like Christmas.

northern Virginia—all over—for auditions. This was before cell phones and GPS, and we were going to some pretty obscure places.

One of my earliest jobs was performing in a television commercial for the local cable company. I jumped around and made silly faces. I loved playing around in front of all the cameras. At that point no one was telling me what to do. Everything I did was all just natural behavior.

When I was eight my mom realized I loved singing, and I entered the world of coaches. It's a big world. I've had lessons in voice, ballet, jazz, tap, gymnastics, and juggling, and coaching sessions in acting. Performing is just like athletics. If you don't practice your sport, you're going to lose your skills.

You definitely need a dedicated parent, or an aunt, uncle, or guardian, to be with you as you go through the training process. In my case, it was my mom. For my first singing lessons, she chose the best-known music school in the Washington, DC, area, so we didn't have to hunt for private voice teachers. You want to make sure that the instructors you find make learning fun, but also challenge you.

We learned later that there's a difference between voice teachers and vocal coaches. Voice teachers train you to sing. Vocal coaches get you ready for auditions by helping to find the right songs for your voice, transposing them into keys that are right for you, and teaching you how to project during the sixteen bars of music you get to sing in an audition—which is usually just one verse or chorus.

At our neighborhood music school, I learned singing techniques and learned about vibrato. We practiced breathing exercises and scales, and we were taught how to project. It was surprising to learn that it takes at least two months to really learn how to sing a song. I learned to practice note by note.

However, I have to admit that I still haven't learned to read music, which is unusual for performers in musical theater. But I want to and intend to—although my dyslexia makes it a challenge. Obviously, it's a huge help for any singer to be able to read scores; it makes it so much easier to learn new songs. Adult professional singers in theater are certainly expected to be able to read music, just like any other musician. And if you can play an instrument, that's a great skill to have on your résumé, too.

A Children's Vocal Coach Speaks

After a career as a singer and dancer, Amelia DeMayo has spent fifteen years training young singers for a multitude of Broadway shows, national tours, opera, films, and commercials. She also helps to organize the Broadway Youth Ensemble, which sings at Lincoln Center and other venues.

Q: *How should a young girl or boy prepare for a career onstage?*

A: There's a phrase you hear in the theater community all the time: *a triple threat.* Casting directors really mean it. They want kids, as well as adults, to be triple threats: a singer, a dancer, and an actor. Parents should get their kids involved right away in musical theater classes, in dance classes. At four years old, if your kids are learning an instrument, it gets good music intonation into their ears. By five, they should already be interested in dancing. I'm a huge fan of tap—it helps with rhythm and coordination. Sometimes I get resistance from boys on dance classes, so I have them go to karate classes two to three times a week. It gets them strong and they stretch.

Q: *What age is optimal to start voice training?*

A: I like to get them by age seven or eight for voice and earlier for dance and music. When I get a ten-year-old, I wish I could have had them two or three years earlier to get them ready for auditions in a professional way.

Q: *What adjustments do you make when working with young singers?*

A: With many young kids, the very first step is very simple: Make them look in the mirror and open their mouths nice and wide. I work with children as young as four and teach them how to make funny sounds in different parts of their voice—a high *whoo* sound and low calling sounds—and to put those sounds onto different notes. I make it a game and we draw their vocal exercises in colored markers. We work on different mouth positions: The *ooh* or fish mouth. An *oh* mouth. A surprise mouth and a lion mouth.

Q: *How long should kids prepare a song before they audition with it?*

A: The shortest amount of time is two weeks. I try to make sure their main audition material is under their belt for a month. Audition songs and repertoire numbers are two different things. Use your same audition song for as long as it works for you. Henry used one favorite song for years and it always brought him work.

Q: *How do you advise youths and their parents?*

A: Young children learn so well by listening. I give their parents certain CDs of singers to listen to. It's very important for parents of younger kids to be in the room during lessons, taking notes or recording, so they can help them practice. The best stage parents become true partners with the child. They should not be critical, however, because children need all the positive support they can get.

Q: *What are the costs for voice coaching?*

A: It depends on where you live. In New York City, for a forty-five-minute lesson, it can range from $65 to about $110. In most music schools, it's around $80 for an hour-long lesson.

Q: *What was special about working with Henry?*

A: Henry was so adorable, he never got cut off at auditions. For five years, he and his mom assumed that sixteen bars meant sixteen full *lines* of music, or about four pages! They didn't know. Henry is a true multiple threat. During a Broadway Kids Care/Broadway Youth Ensemble collaboration at the Tribeca Film Festival, we had Henry doing gymnastics while he was on his wheelie shoes, singing, tapping, and doing handsprings. Anything we asked, he did!

I played a 5-year-old victim in an American Red Cross video titled "Overdosed Infant and Child CPR." The teacher's line was, "Quick, call 911! Henry has stopped breathing!" I appeared in a few more training films for the Red Cross—usually unconscious, drowning, or otherwise injuring myself!

When I was younger, I could hit high notes, low notes, and everything in between. When boys go through puberty, our range narrows for a while as the voice changes. The range later returns, but about an octave lower. Boy sopranos and altos turn into grown-up tenors and baritones and basses. Girls' voices change too, but usually in less dramatic ways. Girls are lucky that way!

I had a hard time memorizing the multiplication tables, so we used special tricks to help me memorize lyrics. I still use these tricks today. First, I read the lyrics through multiple times on the sheet music. I circle any words I have trouble with. The voice coach adds check marks on the music showing me where I'm supposed to take a breath.

My work in commercials helped me in my very first theater audition. When I was seven, I had gotten a script for a Burger King commercial. A short time later, my mom learned about the citywide auditions for all the Washington-area theaters. These are important auditions when casting directors from all the theaters come together and look at actors for all their productions. At the audition, I was the only kid in a long line of adults. I brought down the house acting out the Burger King commercial.

My second Broadway audition was for the national tour of *Beauty and the Beast*. (The first was an open call for *The Lion King* at Howard University, but I didn't get a part.) My mom called a music store and asked for the sheet music for "Where Is Love?" from the musical *Oliver*. The clerk asked, "What key do you want it in?" That's when we learned you could get music customized for your voice. We asked the clerk to send it in a key a little boy might sing in. Luckily, it worked.

Books such as *Broadway Kids' Songs* have practice CDs in the back with music for the songs (like karaoke backing tracks), but each song is set in only one basic key—a key that suits a lot of young voices. There is software available now that will raise or lower the pitch of a song, in the form of a digital audio file, into any key you like. But the best solution is to hire a transposer to copy the sheet music for your audition songs into keys that fit your voice. We asked around to find transposers. They usually charge about $75 per song and it can take up to a week to get the work done.

Dance teachers have given me the most help. Ballet and tap classes are pretty necessary if you want to be in musicals. I started ballet classes at age seven at the Maryland Youth Ballet near my home because it was the only place my mom found that had

The girl who played my sister and I are between shots here in the checkout line, shooting a TV commercial in a brand-new Harris Teeter grocery store in Virginia. I am wearing my lucky shirt, which I wore to most of my auditions and on several jobs for a couple of years. The shoes I'm wearing I wore only at auditions and on jobs, to keep them clean. I was given the shoes after wearing them as part of my costume in a Mattel toys ad.

A Broadway Dance Teacher Speaks, Take 1

Janine Molinari, the owner of Dance Molinari NYC/LA, taught me tap classes for seven years.

Q: *How much time should young dancers devote to practicing outside of their weekly classes?*

A: I hope they'll do thirty minutes a day. The kids bring me notebooks and I write in exercises they should do to stay limber. If they're watching their favorite TV show, I tell them to sit in the butterfly position [on the floor, with their feet together and knees open in a diamond shape], lean over, and count to thirty. Or the first thing in the morning, get their [resistance] bands and stretch along to a song they're trying to learn. They can't learn to do a split or double turn without working on stretching.

Q: *At what age should children start dance lessons?*

A: Seven or eight. Any younger, and their bodies aren't strong enough. At seven, they can start ballet and [the] fundamentals of tap. We won't start leaps and turns until they're nine or ten.

Q: *What is a typical schedule for one of your classes for the youngest dancers?*

A: We start out with thirty minutes of ballet and jazz ballet to music they like—there's a lot of Disney tunes and sometimes they sing along. Then I shut the music off and we switch our shoes to tap. Tapping is playing an instrument. Your feet are drumsticks and the floor is their drum.

Q: *What kind of class schedule do your young performers keep?*

A: They see me one-on-one once a week and maybe one of my assistants for thirty minutes. Then, depending on their age, they take two or more classes on Saturdays in either tap, musical theater, ballet, acrobatics, or music video pop.

Q: *Has the popularity of dance shows on television increased the demand for more advanced moves?*

A: In the past three years, the level of difficulty has skyrocketed. Our first concern is safety, but the kids are asking to do these complicated leaps and turns.

Q: *How can kids prepare for dance auditions?*

A: I make it my business to know every dance in a Broadway show that features kids. Friends who are dance captains and my kids who are in shows share the combinations with me. You want to know the basics before you're in the audition room. But the essential thing is to learn techniques so you can pick up any combinations they throw at you.

Q: *Henry came to you at age ten. Was that late?*

A: Boys can start a little later. But he really focused. In one year, he came so far. He wanted to learn everything. He saw me twirling a baton for someone's *Music Man* audition and he had me teach him how to twirl! He wants to learn everything.

boys-only classes. In fact, at first the classes for boys were free because they were so desperate to have young male dancers.

We couldn't find any tap classes that boys were taking in Washington, so I didn't really start tap classes until I was in New York City for *Beauty and the Beast*. I took both group classes and private lessons in tap dance from age ten until I was sixteen. I also took weekly ballet classes in New York City and voice lessons.

Lessons are expensive and time-consuming. Private classes can cost more than $100 an hour and group lessons $15 and up. If you're a working performer, you can deduct the cost of lessons on your tax return, but it still can be a big cost. And you should practice what you learn in class at home, so that doubles your time commitment. Some instructors let your parent videotape lessons, so you can go over the moves and your technique at home.

It was a lot of trial and error trying to find the right teachers. We went to many classes that didn't work out. At first, we couldn't find a tap teacher in New York who taught kids. A cashier at the Hotel Edison told us about a teacher who did. You should know that there are many classes in many styles of tap, such as jazz tap and rhythm tap, but the one you need for most musicals is called Broadway tap.

Finally, we ended up with a ballet teacher, Finis Jhung, who later worked with the *Billy Elliot* dancers, and a tap teacher, Janine Molinari, who went on to coach the boys who auditioned for *Billy Elliot*. (I worked for years on tap and ballet to be ready for *Billy Elliot*, but by the time auditions began in New York, I was too old for the part. That was a big disappointment.) I had another good ballet teacher in New York, Yuka Kawazu. Yuka's advice? "Students should maintain a steady regimen of classes so that they may gain strength in their technique."

We read trade publications such as *Back Stage* and talked with other parents of kid performers to find out who the good coaches and instructors were.

I started doing gymnastics when I was twelve. I chose floor gym, rather than bar gym, because gymnastics on a bar can't be done in an audition. Janine Molinari's brother, Alex, is a gymnast, so he was the one who taught me to do handsprings, walking handstands, and front and back tucks.

Tap and gymnastic skills really helped when I tried out for *Tarzan* on Broadway. Usually, you never go further than a front roll or flip in an audition. This time, they asked us to walk around on all fours. The audition room was three stories high, and we went up to the ceiling with harnesses on and did free falls to the floor. It was so much fun. We got to climb on ropes and do improv with a ball, pretending we were monkeys. You had to really commit—with all the sounds and chest pounding—or you'd look like an idiot. I didn't get the part, but the audition was a blast.

I added archery to my skills when I was a counselor in a summer day camp, where I was helping to coach a junior production of *Beauty and the Beast*. Because I am naturally curious, I spent time with the archery instructor, learning the basics during downtime for both of us. Then the

With my grandparents on my father's side, Cecil and Barbara Winter-Hodges, at a pub in Suffolk, England, where they live. Cecil was a child actor, and later served in the Royal Air Force during World War II, eventually joining a bomb-disposal unit. My grandfather has a very dry wit—my father thinks I inherited my sense of humor from him.

A Broadway Dance Teacher Speaks, Take 2

 Ray Hesselink, a New York City–based choreographer and director, gave me tap lessons. Here are some of his thoughts about child performers.

Q: *Can you describe any adjustments you've made when you're working with young dancers?*

A: I find children are very impressionable, so I always use words of encouragement when working with them. I also never teach down to kids. Kids are sponges and have the ability to learn way more than we often give them credit for.

Q: *What attributes, in Henry and others, make the teaching experience go smoothly?*

A: Henry loves what he does. My students who succeed are the ones who do it because they have to do it and love to do it. Some attributes are the willingness to take correction, the desire to strive to be better, a positive and joyful outlook on dance and the process of learning, and practice, practice, practice.

Q: *How should a young girl or boy prepare for stints in dance?*

A: Buy a video camera and record every lesson, and practice endlessly. Also, find the right teacher. Do your research. Hire the best. If the child chooses the life of a dancer, the child should be learning many dance disciplines to be prepared at the audition. Also, at the audition, the child should learn how to adapt to the choreographer's needs and styles. Listen closely to any corrections.

Q: *What hazards should they watch out for?*

A: People who promise the world and ask for a lot of money in return. Watch out for the charlatans. Word of mouth is great. Find the instructor with the best students.

Q: *What experiences with Henry illustrate the true life of a working child performer?*

A: Everyone has their own learning process. Some students are visual, some auditory. Henry is slightly dyslexic. I had to restructure the lesson for his abilities. Once you know how the student processes information, then you can be a better teacher. Henry thrived on repetition. Once he had the dance in his muscle memory, he was home free and ready to perform.

On the *Mary Poppins* set with my mother's family (*from left to right*): my aunt Kate, my grandparents Thalia and Dr. Larry Funt, and Aunt Kate's huband, Mike Berman. My entire family, not just my parents, has always supported me. My grandparents saw the show seven times.

archery instructor got sunstroke. When the camp director asked if anyone could handle archery, I raised my hand. (My motto is ALWAYS SAY YES—see chapter five for more on that idea!) The camp gave me some additional instruction and I actually passed the archery instructor's test. Now I have *archery instructor* on my résumé under "Skills." You just never know what a director might want.

Another part-time job I held taught me something new too, but I haven't figured out a way to put it on my résumé. I once helped my cousin with his skylight business, using a harness to climb around on roofs during installations. I guess it's a little like the skills Bert the chimney sweep needs in *Mary Poppins*—he not only cleans chimneys but performs a tap dance number on a harness that enables him to dance his way up and across and back down the entire proscenium arch at the front of the stage! I'm not sure I can dance on the ceiling, but I'm not afraid to try. Maybe I should just say I'm not afraid of heights. Always say yes!

A new sports skill that I'm learning on my own now is free running. It's like urban gymnastics: You run up a ten-foot wall or follow a parkour course, where you run around obstacles. It's an incredible sport. You can see actors using it in films like *Batman*.

I learned magic tricks from books. I've learned several of the accents I do from listening to YouTube segments on Southern, Irish, Yiddish, Scottish, and German accents. On the big productions, there are dialect coaches to help you. In *Chitty Chitty Bang Bang*, where we needed British accents and Vulgarian, a made-up accent, the coach would give the kids and adults notes on cards during rehearsals. She'd also write down certain words and tell you how to say them.

YouTube has also been helpful for some of my performance instruction. If you need to see someone doing something—anything—you can find it on YouTube.

Other offstage jobs in the entertainment world can give you great experience that will help you as a performer. The first time I was hired for any of these gigs, most of these jobs were completely new to me—I didn't even know they existed.

For example, being a reader at auditions is a useful way to understand what casting agents are looking for when they narrow their choices for a part. I was a reader for the young actors who were auditioning for the role of Jane Banks in *Mary Poppins*. During these auditions, I read the lines for "my" part, Jane's brother, Michael.

I was in the room with the casting crew all of the time, so I got to hear all of their comments on the actors who auditioned. At times, they even asked me what I thought of a particular young actor and if I would like working with her.

I did this again for *Billy Elliot*. I had auditioned so many times for that show that the casting people knew me pretty well. They asked me to read Billy's lines with the girls auditioning for the role of the ballet teacher's daughter. I spent a whole day with the creative team, learning their likes and dislikes. This is very valuable information for a young actor to learn—and for actors who think they might someday like to direct.

I also worked as Sandra Bullock's acting partner for an early read-through for the film *Extremely Loud and Incredibly Close*. Sandy grew up in the suburbs of Washington, DC, as I did, and it was really fun to work

An Acrobatics Coach Speaks

 Alex Molinari, an instructor at Prime Time Tumbling in New York City, trained me in "acro," as it's called in the business.

Q: *How should a young girl or boy prepare for the theater?*
A: Versatility is always a key component of success. A performer who can fill any requirement of the show or audition always brings more avenues of success. Strong dance, voice, acting, and acrobatic skills not only open them up for a variety of roles, but also lend themselves to the most important quality, confidence.

Q: *How can children do their best in auditions? What basics do they need to know?*
A: Make sure they know the technique they are performing at auditions. If they attempt a technique that they don't know, or aren't close to performing competently, it compromises their safety, and demonstrates how little they know. It may label them as a liability and represent too great a risk in casting them. A solid base of strong, clean cartwheels, rolls, handstands, walkovers, and handsprings, plus good flexibility, often will get a performer into the door for most roles requiring acro. Lately the dance and talent shows on television seem to be pushing the bar much higher. More shows are requiring higher-level, "exciting" skills. This puts even greater demands on performers.

Q: *What is the toughest part of your job?*
A: It's making the decision to allow a student to perform a technique on their own—without a mat, spotting, or any other apparatus that can keep them from harm. Continued use of such items or spotting creates a reliance on the instructor or the device. At the same time, looking a student in the eye and asking them to perform a task they have never attempted is always a nerve-racking process that never gets less stressful.

Q: *What attributes make learning acrobatics go smoothly?*

A: If we are talking pure Olympian standards, it's fearlessness, explosive athleticism, determination, and a childlike excitement for learning. Henry went through several stages, and the first couple were definitely not explosive athleticism or fearlessness. As he got older, his adult strength and explosiveness set in. He became one of the more advanced students in my New York classes.

Q: *What happens when things go wrong for young performers?*

A: Injuries are the most common, along with the inability to perform a new technique correctly or to perform the technique at all at an audition. I've had young performers come back heartbroken, telling me that they've "failed" in some way. I try to put it in perspective for them. They may feel it's a setback with no recovery, but nothing strengthens determination better than failure. I remind them of what they've learned. When they are prepared, whether they win a part or not, they can feel like a success for what they've achieved.

Q: *What hazards should they watch out for?*

A: Unfortunately, there are false promises from people looking to get ahead on their backs, overpriced training intensives, classes that teach little and prey upon unsuspecting new parents or performers. Every aspect of theater has scams and people with ill intentions, even a director or casting agent who demands too much for a sought-after role simply because they can. One problem is when a performer loses interest in what they are doing. Not every young person who gets into theater is destined to stay in theater. Recognizing burnout is important.

with her. We rehearsed for four days in New York City, but in a different location each day to avoid the photographers who chase stars such as Sandy.

I played Sandy's character's son, Oskar, who is the focus of the film. Oskar has Asperger's syndrome, which is a high-functioning form of autism. He's really smart, but has difficulty connecting with people emotionally, and he has a lot of fears and obsessions. I was actually put in a special-needs class at school for a while with kids who had all kinds of challenges (which was totally inappropriate for a kid with dyslexia—my school was totally clueless about how to help me, though not for lack of trying). The class didn't help me learn to read at all, but it gave me a chance to observe kids with various kinds of learning and emotional problems really close up, and I became good friends with one of the other boys. Even as a little kid, before I ever started acting, I instinctively had that actor's habit of observing human behavior attentively—all kinds of human behavior. That's an important thing for all kid actors to remember: Acting isn't only about good technique or about what you can dig up inside you, in your own feelings; it's about all the things you've stored up from watching and listening to other people in real life.

After a while, the people who were filming the rehearsals started asking me what I thought the character might do or feel and filmed me talking about my ideas for the boy's character, and even for his costumes. I had a lot of suggestions, such as that Oskar would avoid bridges out of fear and would always carry certain items in his backpack, such as a multi-tool, highlighters, and Band-Aids. I thought he might have a gas mask in his room too. They even wanted to buy my own backpack for the movie after seeing me improvise with it! When I watched the film, I saw a lot of my suggestions that had ended up onscreen.

It has been a good lesson for me to learn that you can contribute to the world of theater and film from other places than the stage or screen. I've also learned that my problem, dyslexia, has certain unexpected benefits for me, because it gives me a very good ability to memorize. Since it is often hard for me to learn information by reading, my brain seems to have developed an exceptional ability to retain information from what I *hear*. I am able to concentrate deeply on anything people say, which is perhaps also one reason why I am a good mimic and am able to pick up accents easily.

I've been very fortunate. Thanks to the good training of my coaches, instructors, parents, and my own hard work, my experiences have taken me into nearly every one of the performing arts. I've done commercials, regional and Broadway theater, radio, voice-overs, national tours, and films.

I haven't done what most kids get a chance to do—school musicals and camp theatricals. But recently, I was a camp counselor and coached kids doing *Beauty and the Beast* for their summer musical.

What I learned was that the boys were especially hesitant to act. They whispered together among themselves and were slightly embarrassed. For the most part, the girls jumped right in. My lessons to them were the ones I was taught: stop mumbling, project, be confident onstage. I felt that I was passing along what my many coaches and instructors had taught me.

3

Agents and Managers

Definitely this one! <u>Not!</u>

As in ME—when I was four!

Henry Hodges

I got started in modeling and TV when my mom called a local children's talent manager in Maryland. The manager met me and gave us the name of local photographers who take headshots. (She had no business connection with these photographers, which is an important point. Beware of agents who sell photo services, portfolios, DVD reels, etc.)

I had fun in these photo sessions—smiling, being serious—whatever the photographer asked. We got contact sheets and used a grease pencil to mark the ones we wanted. Now photographers just send the photos by e-mail and you select on your computer the ones you want. You then order individual prints, which cost about a dollar each. When I started out, headshots were almost always black and white, but now pretty much all of them are in color.

We learned that you should wear kid-appropriate clothes for your photos—but no logos. The brand may conflict with a company interested in hiring you. You also don't want a logo detracting attention from *you*. You want to keep your hair and clothes simple for your headshots. No stripes or distracting prints. You shouldn't wear costumes or hold any props.

In addition, don't dress up your photos and résumés. I've seen girls hand in headshots decorated with colored-paper cutouts or scrapbooking accessories or sparkles. They're trying to stand out, but these art-project headshots just make them look like rookies. Agents do not want sparkles all over their papers or laps.

After we got my first photos printed in eight-by-ten size, my mom and I stapled a bio sheet to the back of each one. We used a sample sheet from the agent to fill out the information I included on the sheet. You should include your name, date of birth, height, weight, hair and eye color, experience, training, and special talents. We learned that you don't list your experience by date, but rather put your biggest and best credits at the top. Also, for safety's sake, since you don't know where your headshots and résumé may end up, you don't list your home address or your Social Security number. We put my manager's phone number as my contact.

Here's one of my first résumés.

Henry Hodges

7|17

301-████

Height:	43 inches	
Weight	41 lbs	
Hair:	Brown	
Eyes:	Blue	
DOB	6.1.93	

ON CAMERA, MOVIE:
Mary/Mary	Solid Films	Patrick

ON CAMERA, TV:
Mattel Toys	National	Principal
United Way	National Campaign	Principal
OnePanel.com	National	Principal
Cable Council	Washington-Baltimore	Principal
Food Finds-Holiday Edition	The Food Channel	Cast
American Red Cross	National	Principal

ON CAMERA, INDUSTRIAL:
Infant & Child CPR	American Red Cross	Principal
Lifeguard Training	American Red Cross	Principal

RADIO:
Sesame Place, Elmo's World	East Coast	Principal

PRINT:
Intercontinental Hotels	National	Newspapers/Magazines
Robert Johnson Wood Found.	National	Newspapers/Print
Amtrak	National	Newspapers/Print
Washington Homes	Washington D.C. area	Brochure
Hecht Co./Strawbridge's	East Coast	Catalogue & Newspapers
Wrangler / Timber Creek	National	Catalogue, only child
Zany Brainy	National	Catalogue
Bon Ton	N.E. USA	Mailer
Style Magazine	Baltimore	Fashion Feature
Farwell Photography	National	Promotional

INTERNET:
Timber Creek	www.wrangler.com	Catalogue, only child
OnePanel.com	www.OnePanel.com	Principal

THEATRE:
Spring Festival	Newport School	Principal

TRAINING:
Ballet		
Gymnastics	MD Youth Ballet	2000-2001
Ice Skating	Marva Tots & Teens	2000-2001
Tae Kwan-Do	Cabin John Ice Rink	1998-2001
	Flying Kick Fitness	1998-1999

SPECIAL SKILLS: Singing - Up Tempo/Ballad Cricket, Bicycling, Loves Animals, Soccer, Baseball, Swimming, Basketball, Inline-skates, Skateboarding, Tennis, Can mimic English accent.

My Mom's Notes

My mom, Jane Hodges, offers some practical advice on managing the business aspect of a young performer's career.

Organization is key. I am queen of the notebooks! Keep all receipts. The IRS allows you to deduct travel, food, and hotel expenses for you and your child while you're going on auditions. You also can deduct the cost of lessons, photos, résumés, postage, sheet music, agents' commissions, union dues, theater magazines, and specialized makeup. If you need to hire a friend or relative to accompany your child, you can deduct that cost as a business expense too. I carry envelopes for receipts and write all details on them instantly. You are running a small business and you need to document your expenses.

My mom walking Pucci, our family dog, while I ride my unicycle. When I got the role of Flounder for a run in Sacramento, the first thing I did was Google the city to see if it would be good for unicycle riding. It's a scenic place with a beautiful central park full of palm and pine trees and wide walkways—perfect.

After I started working in New York, my mom sent my headshots to a service that corrects any little defects you may have in your photo, air-brushing out stray hairs or reducing moles. It's all done electronically now, in digital files that you send to the retoucher.

Getting started as a performer should not cost you a lot of money. Some people feel they have to spend big dollars on fancy photographs or a series of lessons and they get ripped off.

This happens because there's a huge desire for fame. Some parents get taken advantage of and pay money for talent showcases where their kids are supposed to be seen by big-time agents. A lot of times the "big" agents never show up. When you see how many kids show up for legitimate auditions, you realize there is little need for agents to regularly attend talent showcases organized by an agent paid by parents.

Two moms of child performers started a group called the BizParentz Foundation to tell other parents about how things work in the entertainment industry and to warn them about scams. Its website, www.bizparentz.org, has information on work permits, trust accounts, child safety, entertainment laws, and an "A+ List" of child performers who have had positive life achievements. Most child actors do very well in life, but the public thinks about the small number of child actors whose crazy lives make the tabloids. The website also explains how legitimate auditions for Disney projects are held, as the Disney name is sometimes used by people with no connection to the company.

The moms who started the website say the need to identify rip-off "talent schools" and to stop uninformed parents from spending thousands chasing dreams is more important than ever. "The money has become huge," Anne Henry, one of the founders of BizParentz, told the Tribune newspapers, speaking about the amounts parents have paid companies that fraudulently promise results. "It's happening on a level we've never seen before."

Even while we were writing this book, prosecutors were addressing this issue nationwide. A glimpse at some of the prosecutions of these supposed talent companies turned up the following:

- A company called The, which now goes by the name The Event, had to pay a fine of $25,000 to the Connecticut attorney general's office after an investigation of its business practices. The company also had to offer refunds to nearly 350 families that had paid for their children to appear in a Stamford, Connecticut, talent competition. The Better Business Bureau (BBB) in Delaware issued an F grade to The because of many complaints, and BBBs in other states and Canada have since issued warnings about the company too. One grandmother had to refinance her house to pay off her credit card, on which she had charged thousands of dollars to send her grand-daughters to a talent showcase in Orlando, Florida.

Watch Out for These Scams

Unfortunately, there are a lot of unscrupulous people preying on young talent. Watch out!

- Avoid people who want you to pay for expensive sets of photos, or demo records or demo reels of you performing. A good school picture or a photo taken by a relative or friend is enough to start with.

- Stay away from modeling and acting academies that charge high fees for required photos, or that direct you to certain high-fee photographers with whom they are connected, or require you to purchase their very expensive leather portfolios to hold your photos.

- Skip showcases that you must pay to appear in, with no guarantee that the supposedly top talent agents will attend.

- Don't fall for companies that advertise on TV and radio, using the names of successful child stars, with the real purpose of selling parents expensive packages of acting workshops.

- In New York City, the WMT Model & Talent Development (aka Model Talent Network, and other names) was fined $908,000 by the city for "advertising services that it did not provide" and "charging customers for photography services as a precondition for jobs that did not exist."

So how do you find the right agent to represent you? Word of mouth is a safe and good way. Find out who each agent you are interested in represents, how long they have been in business, and if they have good contacts with casting directors. Most states require agents to be licensed under the same laws that license employment agencies. So you definitely should check whether an agent is licensed. You can ask professors of theater, dance, and voice at local universities for recommendations of local agents. Study local theater playbills for mentions of agents, or ask the artistic directors of local theater companies for their suggestions.

The two big actors' unions, Actors' Equity Association and the recently merged Screen Actors Guild (SAG)/American Federation of Television and Radio Artists, have searchable lists on their respective websites of agents they have approved, or "franchised," as working with their union rules. Look at their "Find an Agent" section. Local advertising agencies also can tell you what child agents they work with. SAG also has a Young Performers handbook that you can download for free at youngperformers.sag.org.

The weekly *Back Stage* tabloid also publishes periodically updated lists of franchised agents, mostly those working in New York or Los Angeles. The tabloid sells printed labels of agents' addresses for those interested in doing a mass mailing to prospective agents.

You can send your headshot and résumé to agents with a cover letter that says you could be available to travel to their office to meet them. Some agents accept audio and video files or discs. Make sure the performances are short (just one song or dance) and shot or recorded as professionally as you can make them. The agents are very busy and won't have time to watch or listen to a ten-minute tape.

Once you get to an agent's office, the child is usually interviewed alone, without the parents in the interview room. This is done so the agent can see how independent a child is and whether he or she is

I'm so grateful to my New York agent for getting me the audition for the role of Flounder in *The Little Mermaid*. The California Musical Theatre in Sacramento is in the round, so the audience is everywhere you look. This scene took place in one of the aisles at the back of the theater. I loved working in this setting because I could get close to the kids in the less-expensive seats. They were really surprised to see the actors up close. You could see the excitement in their eyes.

genuinely happy to be acting or modeling. The agent may have you read a sample script to see how you handle new material in a cold reading and whether you can take direction.

Agents also attend the "open calls" that theater communities in many cities organize once or twice a year. These open auditions, which typically are free to performers, are a good way to be seen. Bring many copies of your headshot with a résumé attached (stapled together neatly).

If an agent likes you and you like them, you will be asked to sign a contract. Usually, the contract gives the agent 10 percent of your earnings. This is why agents are sometimes called "ten percenters."

Many actors also have managers. Agents submit your name for jobs with casting agents. Managers, who usually take 15 percent of your earnings, take a wider look at your career. If you have a theatrical agent, your manager can call agents in other fields—such as movies and commercials—for you.

If you have both an agent and a manager, you will be giving up 25 percent of your paycheck in commissions. In addition, managers typically do not have to be licensed. The Talent Managers Association, founded in 1954, has a code of ethics. You can view its members at www.talentmanagers.org.

How do these representatives get you work? Typically, producers and directors will send daily lists of character "breakdowns" for upcoming projects to agents and managers by e-mail. A breakdown might say, for example: MALE, TO PLAY 16, WITH BROWN HAIR AND SLIGHT BUILD. The reps then contact their actor clients who might fit the bill.

My mom helps me prepare for auditions and helps me work on my parts. Here we are rehearsing in a Sacramento hotel room. I'm singing, "She treats me like sashimi left over from last week!" Rehearsals at regional theaters are much shorter than Broadway rehearsals. We had only two weeks in Sacramento to put up the whole show. That's fast. After a show opens, I still keep rehearsing on my own, to make my performance tighter. This is typical of the kind of hotel room most actors have on the road. It was my home away from home, so I was happy to have a sunny, palm tree–filled balcony, plus a fridge and microwave. I bring my own hot plate. We made many runs to the farmers' market for local strawberries and peaches and for great tamales from the tamale trucks.

Agents and managers also network and dig around by phone and online to find out how they can get their clients into specific shows. Alert reps are always reading "the trades," usually *Back Stage*, which focuses on New York–area theater, and the national magazine *Variety*. There's also a lot of luck involved—who hears about which projects first.

Your agent will be the one to tell you that you did or didn't get a job. It's called "booking"—as in "You're booked for the InterContinental Hotels ad." You may have a good idea at the audition or prescreening for an audition whether a casting director liked you, but your future employers will communicate only with your agent, not with you or your parents.

Working with an agent or manager is a two-way street. Availability is huge. You have to let your agent know if you're going on vacation, if you've broken your arm—anything, really, that's going on in your life. You have to be able to get yourself to auditions and get there on time, in clean clothes and with your sheet music and headshots. You have to be prepared for last-minute phone calls. And they always seem to be last-minute calls! Staying organized—with a set of clean audition clothes always ready—is a big part of being a performer.

DISNEY *Henry*
THEATRICAL
PRODUCTIONS LTD.

REMINDER
Per conversations with the
Company Manager
we would like to confirm the following:

DISNEY ON BROADWAY –
KIDS PIZZA PARTY!

WHO: All the kids in Disney's *The Lion King,*
Beauty and the Beast, Tarzan and *Mary Poppins*

WHAT: A pizza party!

WHERE: John's Pizzeria
260 West 44th St.
(B/w Bway & 8th)
(212) ███████

WHEN: Wednesday, JAN 24

TIME: After the matinee; 5pm – 7pm

**All the kids will be escorted by the child
wrangler to and from John's Pizzeria. Those
who do not have an evening performance can
be picked up at 7pm.**

QUESTIONS: Call David Scott ████████
Dusty Bennett ████████

© Disney

Tom Schumacher of Disney Theatrical Group and author Ridley Pearson hosted a party in order to talk to child performers in Disney shows about their lives. (Ridley was working on a book for Disney at the time.) After I got home, I wrote Ridley an e-mail with more of my thoughts on the subject. Tom liked my e-mail so much, he held the presses so he could add the text to *How Does the Show Go On?* Later, Disney asked me if I could expand that e-mail into . . . this book!

4

Auditions

Learning to read a script into a microphone is important for radio, TV, and film work—and sometimes for voice-over audition recordings too. Here I am making a sound recording for Fisher-Price See 'n Say toys. I sang several songs about farm animals and made remarks such as "Great job!" and "That's right!" Usually sound studios are freezing cold because the equipment gives off a lot of heat and has to be kept cool or it may malfunction. I always remember to wear a sweatshirt or jacket, even if it is 100 degrees outside.

Auditions are a fact of life. Whether you're trying out for show choir, a place in a college acting program, or a role as understudy on Broadway, you need to learn how to make auditions work for you.

I get energized at auditions. That's not to say I've never gotten nervous. But preparation can give you confidence, and surprisingly, auditions can be fun. They are a chance to show talented people in the business what you can do. If they don't choose you today, what you do in the audition room may help you in the future.

Casting agents typically work for a variety of producers and shows, and they do remember you. A casting agent who didn't choose you at one audition can call your agent and ask you to come in and read for a part in another show. So a good attitude to have is that one purpose of auditions is simply to get yourself in front of as many reputable casting agents as you can. Today's role is not everything!

There are experts you can hire—audition coaches. But most of you will be using your parents or friends to help you "run" or learn lines, rehearse songs, and serve as a sounding board for how you're doing.

It's always best to audition in person, although today many auditions are done in front of video cameras in your agent's office or your own home and e-mailed. Technology helps performers who live far from New York or Los Angeles. Taped auditions are more common for films and TV than for theater. (If you're mailing in an audition CD or demo reel, don't forget to label it. You'd be surprised how many agents receive discs with no ID. They can get separated from the cover letters that are sent with them.)

Putting *unicycle riding* on my résumé is an attention grabber. Casting agents ask me about it a lot. I found a lot of places to ride in Sacramento on my time off from playing Flounder in *The Little Mermaid*. After Sacramento, I was living on a ranch in Los Angeles for a couple of months while

Video auditions let you choose your best "take" and give you total control. But in person, casting directors can ask for more of your talents and better assess your personality and work habits.

I've learned that the unexpected always seems to happen just before an audition. Actors get lost trying to find the casting office, or forget their music, or spill something on their shirt. To avoid last-minute disorganization, I keep a backpack already filled with all the papers and permits I need (see "What's in My Grab-and-Go Backpack?" page 64). Because things can go wrong.

When I was nine, I had my first appointment for an audition for a national show—the touring production of *Beauty and the Beast*. We learned about the audition through another actor, who had heard about it from the show's choreographer. We sent my résumé and headshot to the casting agent in New York City and were given a date and time to show up.

Having a date and time is important. That means the casting agent wants to see you and is expecting you. This is different from the "cattle-call" situations in which a notice in *Back Stage* or elsewhere gives one time and place for anyone to show up. Such auditions are officially named "open calls," and they often result in lines around the block, like the ones you see at *American Idol* auditions.

I'm hardly ever sick, but of course, I got a sore throat the day before my *Beauty and the Beast* audition. As I said, things can go wrong. But I wanted to do it. My mom and I took the train to

auditioning for TV and film roles. That also was an amazing place to unicycle, but one day I slipped on a rock and dislocated my elbow. The injury took a few months to heal. I really was lucky I didn't hit my head. Now I always wear a helmet.

A Broadway Producer Speaks

 Jennifer Maloney, a Broadway producer with Awaken Entertainment, talks about auditioning and casting.

Q: *What are your worries in undertaking a production with child performers?*

A: If you're using children, they're obviously pretty crucial to the production. There's a lot riding on someone who is growing and learning. You can lose time and money, especially in TV, which uses babies and very small children. You've also got uncontrollable elements like voice changes and growth spurts.

Q: *What adjustments have you made for child actors?*

A: In one film, we cast a little boy who got terrified once he was on the set, surrounded by fifty or sixty people. He was cast by our extras-casting people and they might not have spent enough time with him. We cleared the set, but once a child gets into hysteria, it's too much for him.

Q: *What happened?*

A: We called Henry's mom! Even though Henry was two years older than the part, he was in the area and didn't mind acting a little younger. He arrived in twenty-five minutes with all his paperwork in hand. We put him in a costume and got the shot done that day.

Q: *What attributes are most important for a young performer?*

A: That they actually like to perform. When a child walks into a room for casting, can you see that they enjoy it? No hesitancy. We want an open, kidlike spirit. If a child becomes too self-aware that they're doing something cute—or *I'm performing now*—they lose their natural manner. The beauty of children is their willingness to try new things with no baggage.

Q: *What skills should they have?*

A: If they enjoy dance and voice lessons, parents can help them get the skill sets they need. It's a disservice if they go into an audition room where other kids have been trained and they haven't. But it has to be because the kids want it. When I danced as a kid, I did it five days a week because I loved it. But I danced with kids who hated being there. It's difficult to watch a child who is living their parents' dream.

Q: *How did you first meet Henry?*

A: He came to our audition for a rap video. He was so excited that he got to wear camo. It's our job in a casting room to show that you're rooting for the actors to do their best job. Things just totally clicked that day—Henry was so pure and such a delight.

How I Send in Auditions by E-mail

There's a real art to shooting your own auditions to send to casting agents by e-mail. Here's how I do it.

1. I pick a light-colored wall for my background and wear nondistracting clothes. I use incandescent light: no office lights, no fluorescents. You might want to buy a couple of clip-on lights to eliminate shadows from your face. I wear natural makeup. I sit on a sofa or stand, depending on the scene. The reader is four feet away.

2. I fix my video camera on a tripod at a distance of about three feet and first film "a slate," giving my name, my age, and my agent's name. I have the camera focused more tightly on my face during the slate than for the rest of the audition to give the director or producer a really good look at my face. Pulling back for the reading itself allows the viewer to better see my expressions and gestures, the way I get the character into my body even for a video audition.

New York City and stayed in her friend's apartment. I remember the radiator heat was so high it melted my mom's deodorant. It must have helped my throat, however, because in the morning, I felt just well enough to audition. I sang my audition song and performed the two Chip scenes I'd been sent. They gave me suggestions and told me to talk faster. Then, big surprise! They called and asked if I could go on tour in three weeks. My mom and I ended up touring for seven months, one to two weeks per city. I was really glad my throat held out for the audition.

3. After filming, I download the material to iMovie and export it to QuickTime. The filming and editing of a typical "two sides" audition can take up to three hours. (Sides are the pages of dialogue from the show that you are sent before the audition. Sometimes they include condensed versions of passages of dialogue that are longer or otherwise different in the show. If you are already familiar with the show you are auditioning for, make sure you learn the *sides*, not the same material as it appears in the script.)

4. I send the e-mail file to my agent via YouSendIt, a file-sharing service that costs $14.99 a month as of 2012. It allows me to send large video files, rather than taking forever with an e-mail program.

5. If your agent leaves every day at 6:00 p.m., try to get the file in by 3:00 p.m. Call and make sure they have received it and that they've okayed your work. They may want you to send other versions.

Besides trying to stay healthy, there are other rules I've learned for auditions. They are:

- Don't bring food other than energy bars and water. Some casting agencies only allow water in their waiting areas. Some have vending machines, and it's okay to eat their snacks. Especially avoid food with odors, like hamburgers and pizza, and never eat candy that might stain your mouth. The casting people have been working all day, usually without lunch, and it's not nice to come in smelling

What's in My Grab-and-Go Backpack?

I never leave home without:

- A water bottle

- Headshots and résumés stapled together, sealed in a plastic bag

- A small stapler

- A pencil and highlighter

- A copy of my Child Performer Trust Account paperwork, which shows that a financial trust account for my earnings has been set up with a bank

- My Employment Permit for a Child Performer (from the state department of labor in the state where I will be working)

- A copy of my Social Security card

- A copy of my birth certificate

I keep my headshots, copies of my Child Performer Trust Account paperwork, my Employment Permit for a Child Performer, and all the other papers I need for auditions in my backpack. I carry it with me everywhere. Here, I am waveboarding by the Port Authority on my way to ballet class near Times Square. So my ballet shoes, and probably my tap shoes, are in the backpack too. Remember to keep copies at home of all your paperwork, including your audition music. One friend of mine left his backpack on his chair at a McDonald's. When he got back from the soda machine, it was gone. He was sorry to lose his tap shoes, but his audition music and paperwork were much harder to replace.

like grilled cheese and onions. This is the casting agents' home—
be respectful. Don't bring popcorn and make it in the microwave.
They'll hate you for doing that.

- Don't play video games or games on your phone in the waiting
  room. I never do. It's distracting. You need to have your head in the
  game. The casting people—including the receptionists—need to see
  that you're thinking about the audition.
- Audition pianos can be out of tune. Keep the notes and the tempo
  in your head. Keep track of the words and the verse you are on. Be
  "in your song."
- Be prepared to change course or improvise. A director may say,
  "I really like your choices, but I'd like to see you do it this way."
  Or, "That was very nice, but could you do it with more energy?"
- Consider learning some unusual talents to give you an edge. I
  learned how to unicycle, waveboard, and juggle. It took me about
  three weeks, working ten minutes a day, to become good at riding
  a unicycle. I ride it to auditions sometimes—people tend to remember you if you show up on a unicycle. It's a conversation starter. I
  also play the ukulele: One of my audition songs, "Short People," by
  Randy Newman, I sing with my uke. I learned to juggle from Dan
  Jenkins, the actor who played my character's father, Mr. Banks, in
  Mary Poppins. After I left *Mary Poppins*, I went back in the theater
  one day to say hello to friends in the cast, and Dan offered to teach
  me to juggle between shows. He gave me two sets of juggling
  balls. He also taught me and the rest of the *Mary Poppins* kids some
  American Sign Language (the language of deaf people in the United
  States). Both have been very useful, and I'm so grateful to him.
- All these skills and others should be added to your résumé. You
  never know what may strike a casting agent's eye. Maybe the part
  calls for someone who can fly on a trapeze. If you already know
  how, that's a plus.

It was a learning process, finding out what happens after the audition.
Sometimes you find out on the spot that you did or didn't get the part.
Often, you find out through your agent in a few days. Or you might be
called back up to four or five times.

Casting agents don't have time to call everyone who auditions and tell them they weren't chosen. Sometimes, no one is cast and the part is changed or cut from the show. Weeks can roll by. Then, out of the blue, you get the magical call from your agent telling you that you've booked the part!

The thing to remember is if you did your best, that's all you can do. Chalk each audition up as another learning experience that will help prepare you for the next time.

Here are some tips I've learned for different kinds of auditions.

Plays

I start the process by using a highlighter to pick out my lines on my sides. For many auditions, you will be performing your lines with a reader working for the casting director. You don't want to make the mistake of saying any of the reader's lines. Underline any words you have trouble with.

Know that often the reader will read his or her lines in a neutral tone. Don't expect them to play their part with drama, even if it's a dramatic moment. They will simply read the lines in the same way for each person who is auditioning. It's up to you to read it with the right emotion—even if you are not getting the response from the other character that you would in a real production.

You need to dive in headfirst with your lines and make a choice about how to perform them. It might not be the right choice, but if you don't add your special interpretation, you'll fall in the middle and not get chosen. Think about what your character is saying and why. See the scene through the character's eyes.

Vocal Auditions

The song you choose depends on the character you're auditioning for and the musical style of the show. If you're auditioning for Tiny Tim in *A Christmas Carol*, you could sing a short ballad or a traditional Christmas song. These same numbers would not be good if you're auditioning for Simba in *The Lion King*.

Your song should be age appropriate and in a key you can sing in comfortably, and it must be a song you genuinely love to sing. There's a difference of opinion over whether you should audition with a song from the show that is being cast or not. I've auditioned successfully both ways.

Come prepared with both a ballad and an up-tempo song, but know that you probably will only get the chance to sing one or the other. Yet I've had auditions where I've sung four songs. Even if they say, "We'll have the music," bring in your notebook of sheet music for auditions. It's useful to have your music in a thin binder, with each sheet in a nonglare sheet protector. It's easiest for the pianist if you have all your music copied double-sided, and have sheets that fold out to avoid tricky page turns. That way you can just hand your music to the accompanist and it will be easy to put on the piano's music rack. Always remember to say "thank you" at the end of an audition, and

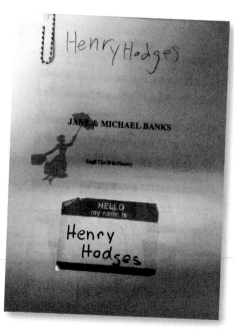

I was given this sheet music for the song "Perfect Nanny" when I auditioned for *Mary Poppins*.

don't forget to thank the pianist on your way out of the room too.

When I was younger, I used popular audition songs such as "Where Is Love?" from *Oliver* and "Gary, Indiana" from *The Music Man*. As I get older, I choose more unusual songs to separate myself from the competition. For girls, it's thought that you should not audition with "Tomorrow" from *Annie* unless you can knock it out of the park. It's been overused.

You want to work on your audition songs a lot. Enjoy the process and focus. Be very solid on them, because there are things you can't control in an audition. Maybe jazz music is coming through the walls from a dance class or the piano is out of tune. You can't let this throw you.

A Vocal Audition Coach Speaks

Michael Lavine is a noted vocal audition coach in New York City who has the distinction of owning one of the largest private collections of Broadway musical sheet music. He works with voice students in the United States, China, and Australia.

Q: *What skills are you trying to impart to a young performer?*

A: I try to teach younger performers to be themselves, and not an idealized "kid" that their parents think they should portray. I think the most successful professional children don't act as much as just be themselves. If I'm working with someone and I catch them "performing," I try to get them to think about what they're doing in their songs so it comes easier to them. It's important that they be able to sing, but that's not my domain as a vocal coach, so I will refer them to voice teachers if I think that can help.

Q: *How do you pick out music and an approach that works for audition pieces for your young clients? What thoughts go into picking a song?*

A: One of the most common complaints I hear from agents and casting directors is that kids sing songs that are way out of their age range. They go with songs because they hear them on the radio or their folks know them, without thinking about what the lyrics are saying about them. I often suggest they read the lyric as a lyric without melody and then tell me why this is the "perfect song" for them. We're usually sitting behind the table thinking, *And I want to work with you because you are a specific kind of boy or a girl*—so find songs that tell me more about you.

Kids under fourteen or fifteen are probably not going to want to sing songs about being in love or they won't get away with it unless it's tongue in cheek, unless it's more of a schoolboy or schoolgirl crush. But a ten-year-old girl will most likely be uncomfortable singing a song about going on a date with a boy. Or it won't make sense to her.

I try to avoid songs that espouse philosophies ("The sun'll come out tomorrow") and that aren't active songs. I avoid what I call "loser songs," songs that present the performer as a loser ("Nobody Does It Like Me," "You Can Always Count on Me," etc.). These are great songs, but they give us a negative impression of the performer.

I try to get them to put themselves behind the audition table looking at someone like them. Would they want to cast someone hearing that song? So many times, kids want to sing current pop songs. Most of them are angst, loser songs. There are many exceptions. I often propose songs by folks like Miley Cyrus or songs from the High School Musical movies. Most of Miley's earlier material is perfect for young kids. At first, the kids cringe, but then when I sing them, they usually like the songs a lot.

Q: *How young is your youngest client? What age do you like to work with the best?*

A: I've coached a few ten-year-olds, but most of my youngest students are in their early teens. I prefer to work with them in their mid- to late teens, as they're working on college auditions and can comprehend things better.

Q: *Is there a difference between boys and girls, regarding the age at which they can grasp your instruction and techniques?*

A: I don't see any difference between boys and girls in comprehension of what I'm teaching, and I *do* see them get it as young as ten. I just began working with a bright ten-year-old last week. She liked some of the songs

Continues . . .

I showed her, and she got them. I love it when they're excited and want to work more.

Q: *What advice do you give young singers regarding work habits and how to practice?*

A: I will make a recording of me singing their songs and then instrumentals for them to practice to. I tell them to warm up, which they learn how to do from a voice teacher. Then memorize the song and start working on it as a monologue. And then practice it in front of a mirror. But most of all, to *do the work*. When they come back to me and have done *nothing*, it's very frustrating, but I'm not surprised. If their parents can instill good work habits in them, it sure helps.

Q: *What makes a successful child singer?*

A: Someone who is being him- or herself, singing appropriate material, and constantly working on improving all aspects of their performance.

Q: *How do you handle voice changes as children age? Can all child singers transition to older songs and roles?*

A: I think ultimately all child singers *can* transition to older songs and roles. However, some of them just don't have the interest after a while. If their parents have pushed them when they were young and they just weren't into it, they should be given the option of deciding this is not for them. That said, the voice changing can be frustrating. I recommend they take some time off and see where their voice goes.

Q: *What about Henry's vocal experience was different? Can you recall any specific help you gave him or how he responded to your instruction?*

A: I know it was frustrating for Henry when his voice started to change. But he was always as professional as I've ever met, even at a young age, so I saw that he seemed to be taking it in stride and immediately attempted to find material that was appropriate for him in his new age and voice type. I do remember he would always be very quick to respond to my direction and I was consistently impressed with his work. I was as hard on him as I was with my Tony-winning students, always calling him on "performing" as opposed to being himself. But I think that's why Henry works so much: He is almost always being himself. He seems very comfortable doing that and making that work in whatever role he is playing.

With Michael Lavine on the *Mary Poppins* set on Broadway. Note that we're in front of the rope put up by the crew to keep performers off the set whenever the theater is dark. Everyone in the cast learns to be very respectful of the set and props. They are very expensive and you can't be playing around with them! The child wranglers instruct all of the kids—principals and understudies—how to move around backstage.

Continues . . .

A Vocal Audition Coach Speaks (continued)

Q: *How long is your typical session with a student and how long do students typically receive your help?*

A: I work in hour-long sessions. Sometimes someone will ask for a longer session, but I don't necessarily recommend that at first. Students have come to me for years. I find it's often cyclical. They come for several weeks or several months. Then perhaps I don't see them again for a while. Then they'll return for another batch of sessions.

Q: *What is your background in musical theory and as an audition coach?*

A: I was an English major at Columbia University. I did study theory there too. Once I graduated, I started coaching students. I've been doing this for almost thirty years now. I often take time off to do shows, but I learn as much about performing and auditioning from doing a show as I do from my teaching. I also do master classes all over the world, particularly in

Come in with your power song and don't stop in the middle if things go wrong. It's about performing the emotion of the song—acting the love.

I keep binders with my sheet music divided into songs I'm currently singing, songs I'm working on, songs I might work on in the future, and songs I have used for auditions in the past but am not using currently. Sometimes we have a special "audition cut" version made of the sheet music for a song, working with a pianist and a voice coach to figure out the best sixteen bars to show off my voice. For example, I might sing only part of one verse, then transition into the last chorus. Often that's all the audition asks for, sixteen bars of a song. You can find sheet music for sixteen-bar excerpts from songs online.

Australia, where I work several times a year at the major conservatories. I've lately been traveling once or twice a year to Shanghai to work at the Shanghai Theatre Academy, too.

Q: *Are there any anecdotes about young performers you have prepared for an audition that you can share? Mistakes to avoid?*

A: One of my favorite experiences lately was coaching my doorman's ten-year-old daughter to prepare her for her audition to get into the Professional Performing Arts School in New York City. She chose "Tomorrow." I had her make flash cards about things she really wanted, such as a dog, and getting into PPAS. While she was singing the song, I would hold up different cards to get her more excited. When her folks came over to hear her sing the song, I watched them gape openmouthed at their daughter. They had no idea she was so talented.

Dance

If you are very young, the purpose of a dance audition often is just to see if you move well. As you get older, auditions become more specific. You and your dance teacher should know the type of dance used in the show. You may want to take extra private and group lessons to brush up and be ready. If it's for a big show, try to find an online video of the choreography. Learn who the choreographer is and look at their bio to see what their style is.

Don't wear tight jeans or baggy clothing. You can't move in jeans. I wear workout pants. Also, don't wear jewelry. And no hats.

If you have them, bring ballet shoes, jazz shoes, tap shoes, and sneakers (or dance sneakers). You might be asked to wear any of them. Maybe you're auditioning for hip-hop, but there's a dream sequence. They can say, "Your résumé shows you've taken ballet. Show us a few turns." You can take off your sneakers and do pirouettes in your socks, but it's better to go over to your bag and pull on your ballet shoes.

Typically, the show's choreographer or their assistant will teach the kids who are auditioning in groups of twenty to thirty. You'll learn a sequence lasting from thirty seconds to two minutes. If you have a hard time

Vocal Terms to Know

Vocal coaches and singing teachers use their own special language to describe sounds. Here are some of the terms I've encountered.

Alliteration—the use of the same consonant sounds in several words in a phrase, a common technique to reinforce meaning in poetry and lyrics, as in such phrases as *time after time* or *playing patty-cake in the park*.

Glottal stop—the closure of the glottis (the vocal folds and the slit-like opening between them in the throat). Glottal stops are essential to articulating the boundaries between words in phrases such as *good dog*, *that time*, or *big girl*.

Key words—the essential words in a lyric—the verbs and nouns and modifiers—rather than linking words such as *and*, *to*, or *the*. Composers shape their melodies and harmonies to reinforce a lyric's key words, and singers usually try to stress certain key words to develop their own interpretation of a song.

picking up dance steps cold, as I do, really pay attention to the beginning and the end. The auditioning team—usually the director, the casting agent, and some of the producers, and often the musical director—will watch from behind a big table at the front of the studio.

If you mess up in the middle of the routine, don't stop. Try to stand near the kids who know the dance. You can follow them out of the corner of your eye if you need to. Keep a smile on your face. Don't apologize. You need the "Yes, I can" attitude, so don't give lame excuses like "My ankle hurts," "My shoes are too tight," or "I didn't sleep last night."

Liquid consonants—consonant sounds that can be prolonged like vowels, especially *L* and *R*. Nasal sounds (*M* and *N* and *NG*) have this quality too. Although lengthening consonants is not part of classical singing technique, in pop and musical theater singing, stressing these sounds can add depth to words such as *love*, *mother*, and *never*.

Onomatopoeia—words whose sounds suggest what they name, such as *crash*, *clang*, and *pop*. Stressing such words can add interest and variety of expression to a song.

Plosives—consonants such as *P*, *B*, *K*, *G*, *T*, and *D*, which are formed with a puff of air. Plosive sounds give words force. You can emphasize them or tone them down, depending on how you want to shape a lyric.

Carrying all the shoes I need in dance auditions—ballet slippers, jazz and tap shoes, and sneakers. You gotta get used to carrying big dance bags! If you look closely you can see a tiny bottle of hand sanitizer attached to my backpack. Cold and flu viruses can race through entire companies of performers, so it's important to disinfect your hands before and after classes and rehearsals.

Don't mingle with your friends at auditions. Be polite, but don't start a big conversation in the middle of someone's dance routine. Once everyone knows the steps, you will often be divided up into smaller groups so that the auditioning team can get a clearer look at each dancer. When your group is standing on the side, waiting your turn to dance, watch for signs of what the people at the table seem to like. You can often tell by their reactions to the other dancers what impresses them, what they're looking for. If you're socializing, you'll miss things like that.

Music Video

Try to find out what kind of styles the musical artist, director, or choreographer has used in their previous videos. Usually, casting directors for music videos are after a very extreme look. Videos go for shock and awe. So if you're thinking about a neon-green Mohawk hairdo, this might be the time to go for it.

The whole point of auditions is to end up in . . . rehearsals! Here, with the rest of the *Mary Poppins* cast in one of our many dance rehearsals. We're watching Gavin Lee as Bert, the chimney sweep, dancing the lead in "Step in Time." I absolutely love rehearsing. There is so much energy going around. The show is actually being created and coming alive through every character in the room. It can be exhausting to take in so much new information. Even if you still feel very excited and "on" at the end of the day, you still have to try to get a lot of sleep to be ready for the next day's rehearsal.

A Casting Agent Speaks

 New York casting agent Jim Carnahan, who casts Broadway shows, major films, television, and touring shows, talks about auditioning.

Q: *What impresses you about a child performer in an audition?*

A: Being absolutely natural. The less coached they are, the more likely they'll be called back or get a part. I've never known a director to respond to a kid who has been drilled on their performance by a parent. It can cost them the part.

Q: *What other mistakes can a parent of a child performer make?*

A: When I was casting for the kids in *Gypsy*, because of time issues, we did something I don't like to do: give callbacks on the spot. So we told each person who auditioned either, "Would you come back in twenty minutes and dance?" or "Thank you very much." One mom stopped me and asked on behalf of her daughter, "Could you call her back? She's missing her grandmother's funeral to be here today." My only reaction was, "Why is she here?" It just seemed wrong. The parents make such a difference that when we were casting [the Broadway musical] *Once*, the director asked to meet with the parents of all the top choices before the final casting decisions were made. Everyone wants to have an easy, collaborative process.

Q: *What advice do you have for aspiring young performers?*

A: Be open to being directed. It's the greatest joy of casting kids to find the natural kids, the ones who are not trained at all. Of course, for a show like

Billy Elliot, the kids had to have that ballet training. But I'm casting *Matilda the Musical* right now (which is scheduled to open on Broadway in April 2013), and the director specifically asked me to find the ones with no acting training.

Q: *Why did you cast Henry as Jeremy Potts in* Chitty Chitty Bang Bang*?*

A: From the minute we saw him, we knew we were casting him. He was the most natural. When you meet someone so smart, inquisitive, and naturally charming, there's nothing like it. There's no artifice.

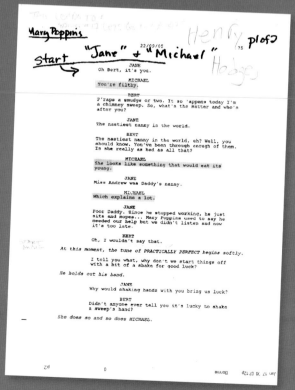

A typical audition side. My dialogue is highlighted in blue.

We spent almost seven weeks in this rehearsal space on 42nd Street in New York City. We are singing and dancing in "Supercalifragilisticexpialidocious" with lead actors Gavin Lee (Bert) and Ashley Brown (Mary Poppins). That particular number was tricky to learn. For starters, it had different steps and arm gestures, based loosely on the sign language of deaf people, for every letter in the title. It was so complicated that just about every day we would start dance rehearsals with "Supercal." It was a big relief for all of us when we finally nailed it. It makes me smile to see that here I am the only one in the photo with my right arm above my left—*wrong!* Practice makes perfect!

Usually you are in a group audition for music videos. A dance captain will teach a group of ten to thirty singers/dancers a dance about three minutes long, comprising up to forty combinations (phrases). You really need to pay attention. The dance captain will run you through the dance a few times. Then the group may be broken into units of five to ten people and you perform the dance for real. It's a lot to learn fast, so concentrate particularly on the beginning and ending, because staying on beat and in the right motion at those moments is most important.

Ads

For both radio and television commercials, you usually need to be lively, happy, and adorable. It matters that you keep on talking with natural energy and that you seem to be happy about what you're saying.

Use a pencil to underline the product's name in the sides and *e-nun-ci-ate* that name clearly. You need to communicate that nothing's cooler or better than the product or experience represented by that one word.

For print ads, you will often be photographed at the audition. In fact, these auditions are called "go see" auditions because the commercial's art director wants to see what you really look like (since some actors may look different in the flesh from their headshots). They also may ask you questions to see if you can take direction during a photo shoot. I've been asked if I can ride a bike or jump rope, just in case the art directors may want that in a shot.

For my first print ad, for Wrangler clothes, the advertising agency director said they picked me because my photograph was the "cutest." But it was an all-day shoot for a catalogue, during which we were moved around the city in an RV. The agency director wanted to meet me in person mainly to determine if I could hold up, as a young child, during a long day with several costume and scene changes.

Television Shows and Films

There is a trend toward realism in TV shows. Watch them and analyze their different styles. What makes the show you want to audition for unique? An audition for *Law & Order* has to be approached differently than one for Nick Jr. Listen to suggestions from the casting agents. They want you to be the one who books the show.

If you have time, try to memorize the sides of the script you've been given so you can act, not read. I've received sides and sent back a video audition the same day, but it takes two or three days to have the lines in your body, in your muscle memory. When you audition in person, you must bring the sides in with you, to show that you are open to the director's suggestions about the scene.

Essential Audition Advice

The most important advice for auditions is: Relax. Be yourself. And remember . . .

- If they stop you after page one of the script, you're not getting the role.

- The longer you're in the audition room, the better the chance they'll remember you. It's a good thing to spend a few seconds with the casting people, conversing about the part, before you start the audition itself. This helps you understand what they're looking for. If the producer or director or casting director asks, I've talked briefly about my schooling or my unicycle. But don't waste their time—they are very busy.

- It's amazing how many jobs I got just by being prepared. I always try to come to auditions with a change of clothes, my binder of sheet music, my résumé, and multiple headshots. The extra clothes help if they want to see you in more than one look. I make sure that I have one pair of dress shoes that look good, especially for auditions for commercials. Know what looks good on you. Advertisers want you to look appealing—you're representing their product.

Your goal is to get the director to remember you by *being* the character. I did a quick magic trick in a movie audition because the script had the character doing card tricks. Instead of an ordinary card trick, I changed one coin into four coins and then back into one.

You do want to look the part. If I'm auditioning for a goofy kid, I might wear a dorky digital watch. Know what looks good on you. I have blue eyes, so for 90 percent of my auditions, I'm going to wear blue to highlight my eyes.

Readings

You can be hired to perform in readings of new plays or musicals. The audition may include one or more scenes from the script and a song from the show. This is all new material, so you have to learn the song for the audition quickly. For readings, you usually need to be available all day on Mondays and during the day on Tuesdays, Thursdays, and Fridays. The rehearsal and performance schedules for readings tend to revolve around show schedules because so many actors in a reading are also likely to be working full-time on a show.

At readings, the actors sit around an oval table and everyone reads their part. Musical readings have rehearsals with the music director as well as with the stage director.

A "staged" reading is usually put on for industry professionals and potential investors. The actors are onstage but with scripts in their hands while they perform. Lots of great plays that are given terrific readings never get produced. Others take years to "hit the boards." That's a down-side for kid actors. By the time the show opens, your character is still ten years old, but you're on your way to college. I've done about twenty-five readings and only two of the projects were produced in time for me to be in the show. Still, readings are a great way to meet and learn from other actors and directors. Readings definitely help you win parts in other projects, and they are great opportunities to network.

5

Always
Say Yes

It's ironic that Mary Poppins measures Jane's and Michael's height in one of our earliest scenes together in the nursery, because our real height was *very* important to us as actors. If we grew just two inches, we could be replaced. We had to regularly line up in the hall outside the dressing rooms to be measured one at a time by someone in stage management. I knew the routine pretty well and tried to make myself as small as possible—bare feet, secretly bent knees, slightly slumpy posture. . . . Inevitably, one of the kids would say, "It's not fair, Henry never grows!" I managed to stay in the show from age 13 to 15. Fortunately, I grew like crazy after that!

There are two places not to be shy about your talents—in auditions and in rehearsals. If a director asks if you can learn German, the answer is "Yes." Can you skateboard? "Yes, I can ride it and jump a foot in the air." Can you do an Israeli accent? Hit a high A? "Yes, and yes." You want to be the actor who can get it done. You can cram-study clips on YouTube to perfect your accents and dialects. I read books to learn magic tricks.

I love to juggle—even while moving—and it's a great thing to put on your résumé. I've watched a lot of YouTube videos on juggling to help me improve. Here I am in Hartford when I was acting in *To Kill a Mockingbird*. I was given the juggling balls by Dan Jenkins, who was my stage father in *Mary Poppins*. He was the one who first taught me how to juggle.

Of course, you have to be honest. Once I was asked if I could do backflips. At the time I couldn't, so my answer was "I can learn." And I did.

When I was very young, I misunderstood an opera director who asked, "Do you sing?" I thought he meant, did I have a singing role in that production? I said no. Later, when it was too late, it was clear he wanted to know if I had the ability to sing, which I did. We'll never know what he might have had in mind for me to sing in that show.

So just say, "Yes." Always.

Taking Direction and "Notes"

The basic hiring decision most casting agents make is whether a child actor can "take direction." They don't want you so rehearsed that you say lines in an unbelievable way. I've found that every director has his or her own way of giving you "notes"—suggestions or criticism about how to improve your performance.

You have to be able to absorb a director's or choreographer's instructions immediately, at every stage of production. The phase of rehearsal

My Favorite Offstage Fun Activities in NYC

I need to rest during my Monday days off in the Big Apple, but I also need to have fun. Here are some of my favorite things to do in NYC.

- Monday Night Magic shows: World-renowned magicians, mind readers, and hypnotists perform in theaters all over town. When I was younger, I was often the only kid in the audience.

- Monday Night with Oscar: showings of Oscar-winning films held in New York City by the Academy of Motion Picture Arts and Sciences

- Skimboarding at Coney Island or Brighton Beach (in Brooklyn)

- Visiting the American Museum of Natural History

With Arnold Martin, owner of a great magic and gag novelties shop on Eighth Avenue, now sadly closed. Arnold is showing me his killer "burning money" wallet.

My Timeline on a Broadway Show Day

Your show-day routine will vary depending on the demands of the show. For example, if you have to dance a lot, you might go to dance class in the morning, or give yourself a barre or other warm-up backstage. If your hair or wig or makeup or costume is complicated, you may have a much earlier call for Hair, Makeup, or Wardrobe than in the timeline below, which is based on my *Mary Poppins* preshow preparations.

Morning: I wake up after eight to ten hours of sleep. Just like an athlete, I have a show-day routine. Whenever the heat is on where I'm staying, I keep a humidifier going twenty-four/seven.

Late morning: I eat a big breakfast with a multivitamin and vitamin C. Sometime during the day, I go over my lines with my mom. I eat small snacks through the day, such as granola bars and apples. I keep a water bottle with me all day and drink lots of water. New York City has awesome water and it comes free with our apartment!

5:00 p.m.: I eat a hamburger or spaghetti with meatballs—something with protein. No dairy—it gobs up my throat.

5:30 p.m.: I sing through a vocalizing routine that I have stored on my home computer for about fifteen minutes, warming up my voice for the night.

6:30 p.m.: I get my backpack and go to the theater on my unicycle or my waveboard. I love candy and tend to pick up a pack of Necco Wafers or a box of Good & Plenty on the way.

7:00 p.m.: I arrive at the theater at least thirty minutes before the first call, which is thirty minutes before the curtain. This is when my child wrangler, the adult who supervises child actors, arrives. I like to get there way early, because stuff can happen—the subway or bus can break down, making you late. I sign in on the call-board, which is usually just inside the stage door. I go into the stretch room, which has mats, so I can get limber before the show.

The half-hour call: Over the backstage loudspeakers, the stage manager makes this announcement: "Good evening. This is your half-hour call. Half hour. Half hour, please." This is when things really start happening backstage. You must have signed the call-board by that time. If you haven't, the stage manager will start calling your cell phone. People will linger maybe another two to three minutes, but then things start moving. I have appointments. I probably have to go down to Hair, meaning the hairdressing department. If I'm wearing a wig for the show, I first have to put on a wig cap. After Hair, I get into my first costume, which is hanging on a rack in my dressing room. I am given a clean undershirt and a pair of socks for every performance, plus usually a clean mic pack (if the show is amplified, as most musicals are today), which is what holds my wireless microphone, strapped behind my back, under the costume.

Dancing backstage with Malcolm Morano, one of the Sewer Children in *Chitty Chitty Bang Bang*. It's fun to goof around, playing games with the other kids during our downtime. The Hilton Theatre is huge and was almost brand new, so the dressing rooms were larger and more modern than in most Broadway theaters. One of the producers, a company called East of Doheney, was a favorite of all the kids. On weekends, they had an ice cream cart come to the theater so everyone could have an ice cream cone before the half-hour call. (Not to be eaten in our costumes!) They also gave us board games to play in our dressing rooms.

Continues . . .

My Timeline on a Broadway Show Day *(continued)*

The 15-minute call: The child wrangler takes me to the makeup room. If you are getting heavy makeup, the makeup folks throw a towel around your neck and get to work. It's your job to sit very still.

5 minutes: The child wrangler takes me to the stage to get my mic checked so that the guys on the soundboard in the theater can verify that my mic is transmitting properly and they can hear me. Then we walk straight into the wings, or onstage if the curtain is down, waiting to hear "Places!" You need to be there at least ninety seconds before you hear, "Places, everyone!"

Even when I was very small, I never minded sitting still to have my hair and makeup done. I find it relaxing, actually. Here I am getting made up to go on as Flounder. Once the makeup designer settled on the look, I was able to do this makeup myself.

The show begins: If the show is a musical, the overture starts. During a play or a musical, the actors aren't called to the stage by name. But in an opera, which may last three hours or more and may be performed in any of several languages, they do page you backstage, as in "Henry Hodges to the stage, please." That's because when the characters are talking and singing in Italian or German or French or Russian, it can be harder to identify your cues in the dialogue and lyrics.

During the show: You want to be ready for your cues at exactly the times you've rehearsed. The wrangler takes you offstage to a spot that's carefully selected in advance. You may need to be near the stage for your next entrance, but not in the way of the other actors, crew, or parts of the set that are stored backstage. Dressers sometimes change your costume in the wings. You can watch the show on monitors at several places backstage and in the greenroom.

Intermission: I go back to the dressing room—often several flights above the stage. Kids usually get the dressing rooms farthest from the stage. In many shows, there may be backstage birthday parties with cake during this break. The parties

Birthdays and other special days are celebrated with cake backstage, often during intermission. Here I am sharing some sugar with *Beauty and the Beast* cast members: (*from left*) Brian O'Brien, Laura Dysarczyk, me, Keith Fortner, and one of the other Chips, Alex Rutherford.

usually are in the greenroom and are announced over the intercom. All the kids must wear robes, to protect our costumes. Sometimes we even have to wear our robes backward for maximum coverage.

Curtain call (bows): After the final curtain—when the curtain closes after the last bow—the wrangler takes me back upstairs to my dressing room. Over the backstage loudspeakers, the stage manager says something like "Thank you, ladies and gentlemen, for a fantastic *Mary Poppins* show number 237." I hang my costume back on its rack and put my undershirt, socks, and mic pack into a laundry bag. I take my makeup off. I go to Hair and the hairdressers take off my wig. I go back to the dressing room, change into my street clothes, pick up my backpack, and sign out as I pass the call-board on my way now through the stage-door exit.

Extras: If there's a question-and-answer session with the audience after the show, I stay to answer questions. If there is a collection for the charity Broadway Cares/ Equity Fights AIDS, I stay in my costume and help collect money at the exits as the audience leaves. I also give backstage tours for friends who come to see the show. Sometimes, celebrities come for a tour. If they have kids, they like to meet the kids in the show. Parties for opening night, closing night, and Broadway events are always held after evening shows, not matinees, so that everyone from the cast and crew can attend.

Postshow: If it is a regular night, I exit the stage door with my wrangler, who makes sure my mom is waiting for me. I then sign autographs for people who wait outside the stage door. Afterward, my mom and I usually walk to our favorite Chinese restaurant, which is on my mom's speed dial. We pick up our dinner and head home.

Here Ellen Marlow and I are trying to get away from a disgruntled employee of the sweets factory, played by Dirk Lumbard, in *Chitty Chitty Bang Bang*. The director told me to really pull away from Dirk, and then to mime stomping on his toe to make him let me go. I'm afraid that several times I really *did* stomp on his foot. Sorry, Dirk!

when the director figures out all the basic stage traffic is called *blocking*. Blocking rehearsals are agony unless everybody knows how to move smoothly around the stage, from entrance to exit. You really have to listen closely at all times.

Some direction of the other aspects of acting can be very literal too—"Do this, do that"—almost like blocking—like "blocking" your voice or gesture or expression. That's easy. But most direction has to do with your character's motivation. Why has he gotten to this point and where does he want to go? The feelings involved are mixed and can be interpreted in many different ways. A director can give you a note on a line and then expand on the thought for five minutes. Pay attention. It's up to you to interpret what the director is talking about.

Rehearsals are a time to learn, so be flexible and keep an open mind. I

My Five Favorite Places
to Eat Between Shows in NYC

On a two-show day—when I have both a matinee and an evening performance—where to have that late lunch/early dinner is a crucial question. Here are some of my favorite between-shows meals:

- Island Burgers & Shakes, in Hell's Kitchen: a hamburger with guacamole and chips

- Café Edison at the Hotel Edison, in Times Square: matzo-ball soup and a triple-decker sandwich

- Ollie's, near Lincoln Center: sweet-and-sour chicken with brown rice

- Renaissance Diner, in Hell's Kitchen: a hot roast beef sandwich and coleslaw. You get a discount with your Actors' Equity card!

- Westway Diner, in the Theater District: a Belgian waffle, two eggs, and turkey sausages

love it when a director gives me notes just like the ones he gives the adult actors. I take it as a compliment. A director once told me, "I want to see a lonesome shadow in your eyes." I thought, *Feel a lonesome shadow?* Onstage that night, I acted distraught. The next day, the director gave me the same note, but added, "Good. This time I want to see more longing." I thought, *Okay, now I can understand where my character is going with this.* The bottom line is, you kind of figure it out yourself and then directors identify what they want when they see it.

Remembering Lines and Becoming Your Character

Memorization is important and isn't easy. You may know the lines, but it takes a leap of faith when you go "off book" and believe you've got them memorized.

One of my tricks is using movement to remember certain lines because your character is alive and would be moving in some way. You step left off a porch or look right at your laughing sister and remember that this

Sometimes being an actor means getting your hair dyed. Some parents and kids say no to this, but my feeling is, you can always dye it back to your natural color. Here I'm getting my character's red hair turned back to my normal brown.

tricky line goes with that movement. It adds muscle memory to the script.

If you don't remember lines, it's often because the dialogue makes jumps in logic. Or your character is talking to himself. Remembering random thoughts is much harder than remembering connected ones. In *To Kill a Mockingbird*, most of the conversation was very literal. One scene led to another. That made it easier for me to remember.

Slow scenes are tough. When there's a lot of pausing and the dialogue is all over the place, don't let your mind wander. In *The Orphans' Home Cycle*, there was a slow scene in which I looked downriver with my bare feet dangling in a trough of water that represented the river. My first reaction was a brain freeze because all I could think was *Yikes! This water is so cold!* I trained myself to continue with what my character would do! I moved my feet as if they were in a slow, warm creek and that helped me go on to my next line.

You have to treat every performance as if it's the last show. Push yourself to be your best. I've always found the first scene is the hardest. Once you get that done, everything falls into place and you relax into the part. When you've really rehearsed the part, you can be confident in it.

Just before I go on, I take thirty seconds to collect myself and say, *All right. Here we go.* I get that adrenaline rush. But if I get that deer-in-the-headlights feeling, I take a few deep breaths.

I know some actors who will stand in the wings and think about their character for fifteen minutes before they go on. The great actor Philip Bosco played my grandpa in *Chitty Chitty Bang Bang*. He always stayed in character even offstage. Other actors literally will be talking to someone about baseball offstage and then go make their entrance.

It's easier to be onstage for most of the show rather than sitting around backstage between scenes. When you don't have much onstage time, you have to get back into the groove mentally before every entrance. Concentration is the most important thing during a show. Sometimes onstage I'll wonder, *Did I miss a line?* Maybe an actor gave me a strange look. Maybe it was just a light that seemed odd. You can overthink things and fumble a line, so you have to stay in the moment.

One key skill I needed was learning to cry on cue. When I was younger, if I had to cry during a scene, I would think of my wonderful pet mouse,

Two scenes in *The Orphans' Home Cycle* at Hartford Stage. As Horace (*top*) reading the newspaper to my employer, played by James DeMarse, whose character is illiterate. In an earlier scene (*bottom*), I played Lloyd, a friend of young Horace (played by Dylan Snyder), whose father has just died. "You're on your own now," I tell him.

Scabbers, who died after he had lived with me for two years. I never had trouble crying. Now that I'm older, I live in my characters more and can feel what they would be feeling.

My safety net is to rehearse, rehearse, rehearse. I work hard at the voice and dance classes I take, reviewing what I want to keep and things I want to improve. Sometimes I practice tongue twisters, like "Red leather, yellow leather, red leather, yellow leather . . ." to help me enunciate and project my voice. It's all about improving your craft.

Theater Etiquette

Most good behavior boils down to being polite. Being on time for rehearsals and performances is key. If you don't arrive thirty minutes before showtime, the stage manager announces your name over the loudspeaker, looking for you. If you don't report within five minutes, they call your cell phone. They may wait another ten minutes, but they'll start preparing your understudy. If you've been late before or don't have time to get into your costume, your understudy will go on.

If there's time to get you into your costume, stage management prefers that to sending out an understudy. They have to announce the switch to an understudy to the audience, and it makes the company look bad.

Sometimes, child actors let stardom go to their heads. Once a girl I was in a show with decided she wasn't going on at the last minute after she jammed her thumb. The understudies hadn't had rehearsals yet and it was really stressful for me and the other actors.

You don't want to be a troublemaker, touching stuff on sets or playing with props. Treat your costume with respect. You do not want to be the kid who spills cranberry juice on your shirt.

Consider every decision you make backstage twice. If you get the vibe that you shouldn't be doing it, don't. You want to stay professional. The adults around you appreciate that. When you're younger, kidlike behavior is more accepted. Just as your parents tolerate whining less and less as you get older, *He's just a kid* loses its power as an excuse.

Being on time also means not missing cues. Your mistakes will show up on the daily production notes. These notes are e-mailed to the producers, director, playwright, etc. The stage manager will write, *Henry Hodges was late for his cue.* (This happened to me once when I was nine and never happened again!)

The stage crew has its own headset communication system that they use to talk to one another without the performers or audience hearing, and the stage manager might say to the soundboard guys, "Yeah, Henry missed that line." You don't want to be the actor who makes mistakes. It is noticed.

The most important rule: Don't give notes to other actors. It's not your job, and really, you're just a kid. That goes double for your parents: Don't let them give notes to anyone. The director doesn't need their help.

Cole Bonenberger was the production stage manager for *The Orphans' Home Cycle* both in Hartford and Off-Broadway. Here he is sitting in the house at the Signature Theatre around Christmastime. Once a show transfers from rehearsal studio to stage, it belongs, especially backstage, not to the director but to the stage manager—who is in fact more like God than Santa Claus. It was simply superhuman to call this show, to give the lighting and sound technicians and stagehands and actors all their cues on headset. Cole was the man of the hour, every hour, through three techs, three dress rehearsals, and all nine hours of the *Cycle*. He never lost his cool, despite the inevitable pressure—a quintessential stage manager.

As Jem in *To Kill a Mockingbird* at Hartford Stage, with Olivia Scott as Scout. This play was my first time playing on a real thrust stage, where you perform with the audience on three sides. In some scenes, we even entered from the lobby through the house. It was an exciting new experience to act with viewers sometimes only arm's length away.

6

Getting Ahead

Winning roles in serious dramas such as *The Orphans' Home Cycle* moved me forward, both artistically and in my career. James DeMarse and I had several scenes together; here we are in our production at Hartford Stage in Connecticut, which transferred Off-Broadway to the Signature Theatre. It was really special working with Jim. I had seen him on Broadway earlier in Horton Foote's *Dividing the Estate*. After that show, I waited outside the theater to ask the cast members to sign my playbill. I told Jim that he was my favorite character in the play. How surprised I was to end up acting with him! What an amazing experience it was to work with *Orphans'* author, Horton Foote, just before his death at age 92. He was soft-spoken and gentle, but he wrote with such emotion. Once I understood the play, it felt so true to me that it was easy to play the part of an abandoned boy. I didn't feel as if I was acting. I felt as though I *was* that boy.

The world of show business is a crowded place. People long to be given a secret way in. In my experience, there was no magic technique, no one lucky break. For me, getting started wasn't about "who you know," because we knew absolutely no one in show business. For me, it was about working hard in voice, dance, and gymnastics classes and studying my lines repeatedly for auditions and shows. That was the way I got a foothold in the profession.

But since I've been working onstage, I've learned some valuable lessons. So here are some of the things I've observed and learned.

My Theater Advice

When you get the part, that's just the beginning. Directors or producers can take it away from you before rehearsals, during rehearsals, even during the show. You've got to stay on top of your game.

One basic is always being five minutes early for any appointment or rehearsal. For performances, I'm there at least half an hour before the half-hour call, and sometimes even earlier. It's rude and disrespectful not to show up on time. It looks really unprofessional to show up late, and people do notice.

Another basic, as I have said, is: Rehearse, rehearse, rehearse. When I'm in shows, I go over the script every day before the show. In *Beauty and the Beast*, I had spoken dialogue in only fifteen or twenty minutes of the show, but my mom and I took an hour and a half to go over the whole show. Every day.

It never should be autopilot. When you rehearse, you want to go all out. That trains you to go all out in performance, so that your voice and body are where you want them to be and your energy doesn't fluctuate.

My mom and I also keep notebooks for every show, with cast lists, scripts, sheet music, and contact numbers. It's very useful when you're looking for audition songs or the name of that assistant stage manager who had good advice for you. You get so caught up in shows that you think you'll never forget anything or anyone in it, but you do.

Taking care of yourself is a big part of your job. You have to be rested, because it's extremely tiring to do a show. I take vitamins every day and

Once we had to evacuate the theater unexpectedly just as we were getting into our costumes during *Beauty and the Beast*. Some crazy person had called in a bomb threat. It was actually kind of fun. We ran out in whatever we were wearing and took a group photo in a nearby park. You can see that most of the cast is only partly in costume. After the whole building was searched, we were allowed back in. The play began almost two hours late.

always wear a scarf in winter. New York is so windy! I also love hats, so I usually have one on as well.

During tours it's particularly tough to stay on schedule. You get into cities at weird hours. You've got to have discipline on the road. My mom and I made a pledge to stop eating French fries because they were becoming an everyday thing. It's easy to order burgers and fries without thinking every time you're in a restaurant.

I've been famous for never getting sick, and I've never missed a show. During *Chitty Chitty Bang Bang*, I did injure my ankle when my shoelaces got caught in a wagon wheel. But a doctor patched me up and I made the next show.

One reason I've been so successful is that I was mostly homeschooled. I didn't have to get up at six thirty in the morning for class and have the stress of going to school and getting exposed to all those germs. I have no idea how the kids who went to normal school did it.

A Stage Mother Speaks:
Advice from My Mom, Jane Hodges

Jane Hodges, my mom, performed in junior high and high school musicals while growing up in suburban Maryland and took some acting lessons at a community theater. But neither she nor anyone else in our family had a connection to professional show business. My mom has willingly devoted years of her life to helping me pursue my career as a professional performer, including homeschooling me with a state-approved curriculum.

As a stage mother, one of my favorite things to do is to sit at the back of the theater and listen to what the actors have to say at the question-and-answer sessions (or "talkbacks") that are held after selected performances. Many of the questions from the audience are repetitive: How do the kids go to school? How do you find out about the auditions? How do the various "stage-magic" props work?

One of my favorite questions is, How did you begin acting? There are as many answers to that question as there are actors. Some actors have famous family members, such as the Redgraves or the Mills. Some actors have parents who are not famous but are in the business themselves and can show them the ropes at an early age. Some actors can never remember wanting to do anything else and work their way through school, community theater, nonunion, and finally union work. Some start acting while in college. Others get into The Juilliard School (the private conservatory of dance, drama, and music at Lincoln Center in New York City) and drop out to be in a Broadway show.

From what I've witnessed, the easiest way to get into the business without a family connection is for a fledgling actor to start young. Take a look at your old *Playbills* and you will see that the child actors are the only ones who have bios with virtually no credits. Unlike all the twenty-somethings just getting through drama school, these kids didn't have to earn points toward their Equity card by working at summer stock theaters, Shakespeare festivals, or cruise ships. (Not that all those

My mom and me on opening night of *The Little Mermaid*.

worthwhile things are not great fun.) These kids had a parent who knew their kid could perform and got them to a Broadway audition. For most roles at that age, all they really have to do is be naturally engaging, and be able to sing, move around the stage, and take direction.

When Henry was little, we treated auditions as fun jobs, so that Henry never knew or cared if he got a part from an audition. All of his auditions were performances—"work"—so he didn't have the pressure of winning or losing. If he got the job, he'd just keep working. If he didn't, there was always another audition that was a fun day of "work" for Henry.

Here is the tricky bit. Getting the part is not the hardest thing about being a kid actor. The hardest part is seeing if the child actually enjoys being an actor. There is no way of knowing if a child of seven or eight is going to want to stick with an actor's life. In a school play, the whole show may last a couple of performances. A professional contract can last six months or even be renewed for two years or longer. It is a parent's job to keep a very close eye on this. One child might thrive on an

Continues . . .

A Stage Mother Speaks:
Advice from My Mom, Jane Hodges *(continued)*

eight-show week and another would rather work two shows and go on his school's field trip. I remember one young actor who was so distraught that he would miss his brother's bar mitzvah that he cried for an hour backstage. Finally, stage management decided to let him take the show off. Your child only has one childhood and you have to make sure he is happy in it.

In one Broadway show, Henry had three understudies. Toward the end of the run, he wanted to take a few shows off so his understudies could have a chance at the part. The stage manager told him he couldn't because he needed to uphold his contract and work every show unless he was sick. The stage manager said, "This is a business, not a school play." I will always remember that meeting. Producers had millions riding on the show and they actually never did make a profit on it.

Henry is lucky because he doesn't dwell on the pressures of the business. He looks forward to auditions, and if he doesn't get the part, he goes on to the next audition. Of course, he loves getting the part and really enjoys the rehearsals, as he thrives on repetition. At each rehearsal he tries to make it closer to where he wants his character to be. He loves being onstage, interacting with the rest of the cast, watching the pros and learning from them. The whole process is fun for him. There is no other place he would rather be.

This is in stark contrast to his earlier life as a student in elementary school. The rigors of the actor's life are a piece of cake because he actually understands and enjoys what he is doing. As a student, Henry's dyslexia defined him. At school he was tested and "coded" and he was often treated as if he had a low IQ. Many of Henry's teachers were well intentioned and a couple worked with him on their own time before school, after school, and even in the summer. He simply could not read or write sentences or consistently add or subtract numbers. His teachers tried, but it was a futile effort.

Every day at school was the same. So, when Henry started acting, it was the first time he realized he could excel at something without reading and writing. He was failing so miserably at school. The last straw for me was when he got a "needs improvement" in his elementary music class because he couldn't follow the bouncing Mickey Mouse ears above the words to a Disney music video. Within months of leaving that class, Henry was singing solos on the national tour of a Disney Broadway show. He is naturally inquisitive and learns by watching and listening. This way of learning clicked for him.

When Henry went on the road at nine years old, he talked on the bus with the rest of the cast and found out that many of them had learning issues too. He finally knew he was not alone and that many successful actors had also had a hard time at school. There is a long list of famous figures in show business who weren't the top in their class, such as Daniel Radcliffe, Whoopi Goldberg, Ryan Gosling, and Cameron Diaz—not to mention Walt Disney!

If Henry's story were not true, I don't think people would believe it. I think my son really was destined to be a performer, and that acting really did save his life. In Henry's case, that's not an exaggeration or a mere figure of speech. When Henry was little, he often woke up shrieking from nightmares, night after night: The nightmares vanished the day he started to work. It seemed that some energy inside him finally had somewhere to go.

Three essential pieces of practical advice for any stage mother or father:

- During auditions, the door is closed and parents must wait outside. Before it shuts, you have to make your child comfortable and make sure the experience will be fun.

Continues . . .

A Stage Mother Speaks:
Advice from My Mom, Jane Hodges *(continued)*

- You want to be the invisible parent. Don't push the stage manager, the costumer, or the ushers. Don't ask for free tickets, or to watch rehearsals, or for an extra copy of the script.

- You've done your job if your child is happy, no matter what the outcome of an audition, show, rehearsal, or photo shoot.

Just remember, your commitment to the show is your whole family's commitment too. Think seriously about what this means to everyone's life. Unless you already live in the New York City or Los Angeles area, you (or a guardian) have to be near the stage or film set for the duration of the contract. That often means leaving your job, finding an affordable place to live, organizing your child's schooling after rehearsals are over, and juggling everything else that is going on at home by long distance. That is just for starters. Do not underestimate how much time, effort, and money this will take. This is another reason the talent pool in young age groups is probably smaller than you think.

If staying healthy keeps you in a show, surprise! You can be so healthy that you grow out of your character. As a kid, you are measured often by stage management. If you grow two inches above your height as measured on the date of your first rehearsal, that gives the company the option to release you from your contract early. Contracts typically last six months and are then either renewed or dropped.

Normally, little kids want to be bigger. Not so in the theater. If the expensive costume the designers had made for the show no longer fits, a smaller kid comes in to replace you. In *Mary Poppins*, my shoes were

> Notwithstanding anything to the contrary herein, it is understood and agreed as follows:
>
> **1. JUVENILE ACTOR**
>
> > **SPECIFIC GROWTH CLAUSE.** It is hereby acknowledged that Actor currently weighs 60 pounds and is 54 inches in height. Producer shall have the right, but not the obligation, to terminate this agreement with no less than two (2) weeks' written notice without regard to Rule 70D ("Just Cause") of the Production Contract, should any of the following occur: (a) actor achieves a weight gain of fifteen (15) or more pounds and/or a height increase of two (2) or more inches; (b) in Producer's opinion, in consultation with the Director, the Actor's physical development has caused the Actor to "outgrow" the role; and (c) in the Musical Supervisor's and/or Musical Director's opinion, Actor's physical development has caused the Actor's voice to change rendering Actor unable to execute properly the musical material of the role.
>
> Except to the extent modified by the foregoing, all other terms and conditions of the original Production Contract between Actor and Producer dated May 15, 2006 shall remain in full force and effect.

This is the growth clause from my contract for *Mary Poppins*. The producer can terminate your contract if your height, weight, look, or voice changes.

handmade and formed to my feet—and they cost $800. The pajamas in *Chitty Chitty Bang Bang* were made of cashmere. You're hired to fit into the original costume so that everyone looks like the actor who played their character in the original cast.

In the theater, you want everyone to be your friend. The casting agent's boyfriend will be in the chorus of a show you want, and if you're on good terms with the agent, she'll be likely to ask her boyfriend about whether you'd suit the show.

Here's an example of why, especially as a child actor, you want to be respectful to everyone. You should know that the stage manager is the director in the weeks and months after the director leaves once a show has opened. That was new to me. I thought directors were at the show every night. No. They leave after opening night and come back just occasionally to give notes and see that the actors haven't slipped. It's the stage managers who can decide if you go or stay.

So, think of yourself as a professional person. It's a classic mistake to be snappy and rude to the dressers, crew, lighting guys, or teachers. Some kids are only nice to the stars, but the truth is that the stars usually don't have that much say about who is in the cast.

Another myth is that because you're all kids, you'll get along with all the other child actors. Parents don't remember that when they were in school, they didn't get along with everyone. In every show, there are always one or two kids who are hard to take. The ones, for example, who say, "Hope you don't miss that line," right before you go onstage. Or, "Wow, that note sounded funny." Don't think about them, because it will mess up your performance.

One child actor in *Beauty and the Beast* had a weird habit of cutting up my possessions in the dressing room while I was onstage. He'd cut my shoelaces, one of my pictures on my dressing room mirror, even strings on the yo-yos that my mom bought for both of us to play with. (He only cut *my* strings, however.) He even told our child wrangler and me that he saw someone he didn't recognize walk into our empty dressing room with a pair of scissors and then walk out. It was so sneaky and strange. The stage staff didn't want to deal with it, so we just learned not to bring my things into the theater. I think the kid was just stressed, but we'll never know. He later got a part in a touring production, but left that show within weeks. . . .

The lesson is that kid performers can have emotional baggage and problems just as any adult actor can. It's just that kids tend to get lumped together in a way that adults rarely are. And kids are seen to be more flexible and willing to go along with things.

Parents make the difference. Although child performers have wranglers who take care of us backstage and make sure we get our cues, it is really important to have a parent around (but not backstage). My mom is my secret weapon. She can see what I can't. It helps to have an extra pair of eyes out in the audience. You'd be surprised what my mom knows—she's a great acting coach. She's the unfair advantage I have over everyone. I get great tips, for free, and I listen to them. Stage managers have told my mom she's the best stage mom they've ever met. That means she's not pushy and doesn't interfere. It made her tear up.

PLAYBILL

NEIL SIMON THEATRE

GYPSY OF THE YE...

WWW.PLAYBILL.COM

BENEFIT ESP1206E

NO REFUNDS/NO EXCHANGES
GYPSY OF THE YEAR
NEIL SIMON THEATRE
250 W. 52ND ST, NYC
MON DEC 6, 2004 4:30PM

<u>PLEASE POST</u> – <u>IMPORTANT INFORMATION</u>

TO: All GYPSY Presentation Coordinators
FROM: Broadway Cares/Equity Fights AIDS
DATE: 11/26/04
RE: Rehearsal Schedule for GYPSY Competition

SHOW: BEAUTY AND THE BEAST

THURSDAY, DECEMBER 2, 2004
Director's Preview   Location: Ripley Greer Rehearsal Studios
                                                  520 Eighth Ave., 16th Floor
                                                  Studio 16L

Each show will have **15 minutes** to present their number and go over details such as lighting
and sound. Expect your total time with us to be about 30 minutes. Please:
1) Remember the <u>3 minute time limit</u>. We will be timing the numbers on this day and we
   will make cuts if you are over 3 minutes.
2) As many people as possible all people participating in the number should attend.
3) Bring a revised script with you.

Your call time is: ___4:00 PM___

FRIDAY, DECEMBER 3, 2004
Technical Rehearsal   Location: The Neil Simon Theatre
                                                  250 West 52nd Street

Each show will have **10 minutes onstage** to tech their presentation (lights, no sound). Since
this is a technical rehearsal, only the director/group leader for the number should attend.
Expect your total time at the theatre to be about 30-45 minutes. Enter through the alley
doors, just east of the main lobby doors. Please do not use the stage door.

Your call time is: ___11:00 AM___

MONDAY, DECEMBER 6, 2004
Performance 4:30   Location: The Neil Simon Theatre
                                                  250 West 52nd Street

Each show will have **10 minutes onstage** to rehearse their 3 minute number with all
technical elements. All individuals in the presentation should be present. Expect your total
time at the theatre for this rehearsal to be about 45 minutes. Enter through the alley doors,
just east of the main lobby doors. Please do not use the stage door. All acts need to be at
the theatre for the performance by half hour.

Your call time is: ___10:40 AM___

TUESDAY, DECEMBER 7, 2004
Performance 2:00   Location: The Neil Simon Theatre
                                                  250 West 52nd Street

Call times for the 2:00 Performance will be determined on Monday, December 6th. Note that
the show begins at 2:00 PM – **2 and a half hours earlier** than Monday's show.

Thank you!

I performed many times in the annual Gypsy of the Year benefit that Broadway Cares/Equity Fights puts on. Here's some of my memorabilia from the show in 2004, when I did a solo parody number based on *Beauty and the Beast*.

7

School Must
Go On

I did my schoolwork in all sorts of places. Here is Anne Marie Hurlbut, my child wrangler and teacher for the *Beauty and the Beast* tour, helping me with a science project, assembling a robot alarm clock. It looked a bit like Cogsworth the clock, a character in *Beauty*. For me, being tutored on the road was *way* better than sitting in a classroom all day. There were only two kids in the cast, so we got a lot of individual attention from Anne Marie. We learned about the areas we were traveling through. Lewis and Clark explored the rivers in much of the Midwest where we toured. Before we left on tour, my mom also ordered a book on each state we would visit. She would read the book to me in the bus on our way from one state to the next. We also got to visit local museums and destinations, such as the Indianapolis 500 racetack and the Motown recording studios in Detroit. I had traveled very little before the *Beauty* tour. It opened up a whole new world to me.

I t's a basic for kids—school comes first. No matter that you're climbing on a touring show's bus to start a seven-month run, you're not going to escape the classroom. State laws require you to continue your studies each day, whether you're performing in your hometown or on the road. I've done homework in dressing rooms, by hotel pools, on airplanes, and in buses.

The demand for temporary schools for young actors, singers, athletes, and circus performers prompted the creation in 1982 of a company, On Location Education. It now has offices in New York, California, Florida, Louisiana, Connecticut, and Pennsylvania. The company supplies on-set tutors for films and television, studio teachers for theaters, and teachers who travel with touring shows. Its founder, Alan Simon, also started the School for Young Performers, which is a private school without walls for kindergarten through twelfth grade in New York City. Students enroll and receive guides on course work and tutoring. Kids must bring their own

Lessons from One of My Backstage Teachers

Brooklyn-born Muriel Kester taught public school for thirty-five years in New York City before retiring to teach young performers on Broadway, in films, and in the circus. She has spent the last sixteen years conducting classes in theaters and rehearsal rooms and on movie sets.

Q: *How are classes conducted?*

A: Students must be in classes fifteen hours a week. They're scheduled for a nine-hour day when they're rehearsing, and I pull them out when they're not being used. The shows rent us a room in rehearsal studios. In theaters,

My elementary school classmates were really happy for me when I won the *Beauty and the Beast* part. They had a party for me with balloons and cake. Here I am outside my elementary school in Bethesda, MD, on my last day in school. My neighborhood friends came to see me in many of my shows on Broadway and I kept in touch with them at birthday and swim parties.

books, but you get good advice on what ones to buy for your grade level. Alan's company also works with private families who travel a lot and with circus kids.

Tutors from On Location Education came to the theaters I worked in and would hold classes for three to four hours every day. In New York, the theaters give us space for a classroom. On tour, it would usually be a room in our hotel or the theater. The tutors work with your teachers back

we're usually in a dressing room or a greenroom. On film sets, we're in a wardrobe or honey wagon [restroom] trailer. I can teach up to ten kids at a time, from kindergarten to high school.

Q: *How do the kids keep up with their home curriculum?*

A: We work with a child's home school to get their lessons either e-mailed or picked up by parents. Sometimes I grade their work, sometimes the school does.

Continues . . .

Lessons from One of My
Backstage Teachers *(continued)*

Q: *How has technology changed schooling for young performers?*

A: Access to the internet has given us a library, books, and the ability to do research. Most of the children have laptops now. Almost all the theaters now have Wi-Fi.

Q: *Where's the strangest place you've held classes?*

A: For one production of *Gypsy* the dressing rooms weren't ready, so we had to use the ladies' lounge. We've also used the orchestra's greenroom. The musicians were very quiet when they came in to get their instruments.

Q: *What do you do for physical education?*

A: Most of these kids are dancing, so that's covered. I took one group of kids from *Gypsy* into Shubert Alley and they jumped rope, with the show's choreographer holding the rope and Bernadette Peters [the star] joining in. Sometimes we'll get consent forms signed by the parents and work outdoors in a park.

Q: *Are classes for young performers an easy way to get through school?*

A: Not at all. Sometimes after rehearsals, after all the other actors and actresses have gone home, the kids stay for two more hours in class. [For New York City theater productions] we only tutor them through rehearsals, previews, and one week after opening. After that, they return to their home schools and attend classes there during the day and perform on Broadway at night. Broadway shows end at about 10:45 p.m. and many of those kids live in New Jersey or upstate New York. That's why they're doing their homework in their dressing rooms.

Q: *Do most of the child actors complete their schooling?*

A: Almost all go through high school, and many go on to college. But 75 percent of them don't continue as performers after their teen years. Once they grow, or their voices change, there aren't many roles until they're young adults. So many of them leave for high school and college. Some come back to the business. Others have a different life and don't return. Henry was one of the lucky ones who made the transition.

Q: *Do you teach every type of class?*

A: No. The very advanced science courses require a specialist to come in. But I do all basic classes, plus beginning Spanish and French. Once, I was tutoring one performer who was the spelling bee champion for New Jersey; I was prepping her for the National Spelling Bee in Washington, DC.

Q: *Are there any special perks to being a show teacher?*

A: We get tickets to opening night and to the cast party. And my name is in the playbill! The best perk is getting to work one-on-one with these extremely talented kids.

About to join the *Beauty* cast on board an airplane to fly between cities on tour. I loved flying because you're there with all your friends—it was kind of like a class field trip. On tour, as soon as the last curtain goes down, the crew is there to "strike" (take down) the set. They also pack up our classroom materials, which are either in a room at the theater or at the hotel. The school materials are usually packed last so they can come first off the truck, allowing us to have class while the crew is unloading and setting up. While the cast is asleep, the crew is packing the set into huge 14-wheeler trucks, which are immediately driven to the next city. The crew is driven there in a special RV with small sleeping compartments. That way, they arrive rested, ready to put up the set again. The cast either flies or takes a bus to the next city and often has a day off (called a *golden day*) while the crew is hard at work. You get to check in to your new hotel room and run around to see what the new city looks like.

Long bus rides between cities are ideal for doing homework. Here I'm reading lessons on my computer. My mom got curriculum guides from schools that teach thousands of kids in unusual classrooms in the U.S. and overseas. Learning on the bus was relaxing because I could look out the window, hear the hum of the motor, and enjoy the ride. Our journey was always broken by a lunch break along the way. It was fun to be able to eat with the cast in a new place every day. Usually, it was a fast-food restaurant. Before the tour I had hardly ever eaten fast food, so I loved being able to order anything in those places that I wanted! However, I soon learned that I needed a much healthier diet to keep me going, so I started to choose the healthiest items available wherever we were.

With my Morse code experiment in our hotel room in Detroit while on tour with *Beauty*.

home to coordinate what you're learning. In *Mary Poppins*, for example, the girls in the show were taking French in their schools at home, so the show hired a French tutor for them.

When we're on tour, our classroom materials are packed up and crated along with the costumes and sets and sent by either plane or truck to every city. We also are allowed to "bank" school hours by doing extra time, so that we can have free hours to be tourists in the cities we visit. You also bank hours in preparation for long days, such as dress rehearsals, or long film shoots.

Our teachers are very creative at presenting our classes. I've done science experiments in makeup rooms and learned ecology from outdoor walks and explorations.

My parents also coordinated my school progress with my home county's board of education, handing in my work twice a year to be evaluated. My mom followed the county's grade-level guides for my homeschooling and got textbooks from libraries and other schools. I had to pass tough subject-matter tests in order to receive my high school diploma, which I'm happy to say that I earned. I'm now taking courses at a local Maryland college between shows.

The internet has made long-distance education much easier. Kids have access to terrific online lessons and books, and we can Skype with teachers and other experts on the road. You still have to have the discipline to do homework, but I've loved the freedom of not sitting behind a school desk.

Like many show kids, I can spend as much time in performance classes as I do in academic classes. They both require attention and practice.

Making muscles like Gaston with my pals at a Valentine's Day party backstage while on tour for *Beauty and the Beast*.

In rehearsal with Sir Richard Eyre, director of *Mary Poppins*, and other kids in the cast. Richard is a great director, always open to hearing actors' ideas, even *kid* actors' ideas. But he always maintained a very clear vision of what he wanted our characters' arcs to be, the journey he wanted us to take from the beginning to the end of the show. Unlike the children in the movie, Richard saw us as truly unhappy at first, lonely and isolated from our parents. At the end, he was looking for a bittersweet feeling, with the entire Banks family looking at the world through different eyes. I'd work with Richard again in a heartbeat.

8

Being a Kid— Acting Like a Pro

Most kids on Broadway have been in local productions, school plays, and camp shows. And in all those, you can believe they've been the star, the focus. When they get to a professional production, they're still good, but they're not the best. If they're expecting constant praise, they're not going to get it.

I had to learn to accept criticism. My first touring show was *Beauty and the Beast* and I played Chip, a teacup. At the end, I ran across the stage as a human again, not as a teacup. My last line was, "Do I still have to sleep in the cupboard?" I took my time saying the line because I had gotten a note from the director telling me to make that line really clear. But the delay bothered the conductor. It threw off the orchestra for the beginning of the finale.

Here I am in my Chip cup and "blacks" in a dressing room on tour with the other Chip in the show, Alex Rutherford, in *Beauty and the Beast.*

I got a note from the conductor. Because I was taking too long to say the line, he was having to add another loop of the music, an extra four bars. The conductor gave me the note four times to speed up. I almost didn't get invited to be in the Broadway production because of it. Sometimes you get notes that conflict, and I was still thinking about my director's note to make the line clear. In this case, I should have just listened to the conductor the first time.

Every show has a different vibe, but we all try to keep the drama on the stage, not backstage. I violated this one time, and boy, was I sorry.

In *Chitty Chitty Bang Bang*, the amazing Raúl Esparza played a kooky mad-scientist father beloved by his kids. During rehearsals, Raúl taught me bits of magic, sleight of hand, and hat tricks that he used in the show. He'd spray me with a water gun, make funny faces, and just generally goof off, all in the name of fun.

One day, I decided to retaliate. I was in my favorite magic shop on Eighth Avenue in New York City and bought something I thought was certain to make Raúl laugh. Just before one Wednesday-night show, I snuck into his dressing room and sprayed two squirts of Fart in a Can in it.

Two minutes later, there was an announcement over the backstage loudspeaker. "Whoever is spraying that stuff, please stop!" My heart sank. I walked out of my dressing room to discover that even the hallway, which was very far from Raúl's dressing room, smelled terrible as well.

Immediately, I went to the stage manager and admitted what I had done. Soon, the ushers began to complain about the smell in the seating area. The 1,932-seat Hilton Theatre (now the Foxwoods Theatre) smelled like Fart in a Can!

I kept thinking, *This can't be happening. It was just a spritz!*

During intermission, I apologized over the loudspeaker to everyone backstage. I then went from dressing room to dressing room, telling everyone I was sorry.

Everything in Raúl's dressing room had to be dry-cleaned, washed, or scrubbed, including all his costumes, the new wall-to-wall carpet, sofa, and chair. This could have been a huge problem for me, but Raúl was very nice about it, and so were the stage management and the crew.

It really taught me not to mess around. Whenever we cross paths, the cast and crew of *Chitty* still give me a hard time about it.

A Director Speaks

English actress Jennifer Crier Johnston was supernumerary director (director of extras) for eight years at the Washington National Opera and has lots of experience with child actors. She worked with me when I performed in operas there.

Q: *Can you describe any adjustments you've made in rehearsal or performance when you're working with young actors?*

A: There are only so many scheduling changes that can be made, since there are so many other performers and musicians involved. In early rehearsals, we could sometimes rehearse the children first and then let them go. Day rehearsals were no problem. But once we were into complete run-throughs, it was necessary to run the show from the top in the evenings.

Q: *What attributes, in Henry and others, make the experience go smoothly?*

A: Henry always came to rehearsal well rested. It is very important that the parents do not push their children too far. Parents need to feed them healthy food and nonsugar-filled snacks and allow for a rest before they come to a rehearsal. This is not always possible with school. But often in the dressing room there would be a bench or little bed for catnaps.

Q: *Can you give examples of when things went wrong with young performers and the advice you'd give to make sure there aren't repeats?*

A: There was one occasion when I was casting for the Mariinsky Theatre [formerly known as the Kirov] and I had to replace one of the little boys who was portraying one of Macduff's sons in *Macbeth* [when the Mariinsky company appeared at the Kennedy Center]. It started when the mother of a little girl who was portraying a dead princess insisted on brushing the girl's hair and coming up to the stage with her. Union rules do not allow parents to accompany their children to the stage. That is why we have assistant stage managers and child wranglers and dressers and casting directors.

Despite being told of the correct procedure, this parent insisted on accompanying her daughter. When advised of the union rules, she suggested a rider be written to cover her. This was a dress rehearsal, so we let it pass. The next morning I received a message that she was pulling her daughter from the production and also her son, who was one of Macduff's children.

I do remember Henry's mother's response when I called her—what time and where do you need Henry? They arrived early so we could fit Henry into the existing leather outfit, complete with [a] gold circlet for the head. He and seven other boys portraying Macduff's sons were in the middle of the stage following frantic hand signals. This was the Mariinsky/Kirov and everything was in Russian! At the curtain call, the children took their bow and Henry's circlet slipped down over his face. The audience and the entire cast laughed and applauded. Henry was a hero that evening.

Q: *How should a young girl or boy prepare for stints in the theater?*

A: Obviously, children who want to make a living in the theater need to be trained. One of the problems today is that too many wannabes watch *American Idol* and think they can just get up and sing. Nowadays it is not sufficient to be a good actor, and move well, and put over a song well; one has to be able to sing, dance, and act, and if possible, play an instrument.

Henry took dancing and fencing. The fact that Henry was small and able to play very young roles would not last forever. If a child actor wants to continue, then they must hone their skills.

Continues . . .

A Director Speaks (continued)

Children should take advantage of the many classes and summer camps that offer training in the theater. I am often involved with summer camps where children are given complete instructions as to what to prepare for in initial auditions. They and their parents frequently do not pay enough attention to these instructions.

It is also important for children to be aware of classic plays and films. When I was growing up, close to London, I was fortunate to be able to pop up and see a lot of good theater, but nowadays children can take advantage of Netflix, etc., to see excellent past performances.

Children should always bring their homework with them and other books or things to keep them busy through the often-long rehearsals. It is important that children keep their energy high and that they do not consume high-sugar drinks, as they give them a false high.

I often refer anxious parents to the novel *Ballet Shoes*, by Noel Streatfeild, which gives them practical insight into children in the theater.

Q: *What hazards should children watch out for?*

A: Few people think about tripping over cables. No flip-flops allowed! Children should know that the theater staff—stage managers, dressers, etc., want them to succeed, so it is always good to get to know them and treat them with respect, since they have been in the business for a long time. Many of them were child actors themselves.

Q: *What experiences with Henry illustrate the true life of a working child actor?*

A: Henry was playing the young boy in the opera *Idomeneo* and his costume was the size of a bathing suit, with bare chest and bare feet. So Henry

My limp and gory body was carried out of the mouth of the giant mask of the sea god Neptune and deposited on the "stone" (actually, very *cold* Styrofoam) altar in this scene in *Idomeneo*. The director and star, Placido Domingo, is at the far right.

would putter around backstage in warm, fluffy slippers and also wore them up to the stage from the dressing rooms. I would frequently accompany him, but this particular day I did not. And so Henry appeared onstage, being carried by Placido Domingo, wearing very out-of-character fluffy slippers.

When we were performing *Madame Butterfly*, it was necessary to cast four little boys so that at each performance we would have one actor and a spare. For one performance we had scheduled a pair of twins—both of whom developed chicken pox. We brought in one of the other two boys, but his standby was also sick. So a call to Jane Hodges elicited what became a customary greeting when she saw my ID on her phone: "When? And where?" Henry was all set to go on in case the young boy of the day fell sick.

Continues . . .

A Director Speaks *(continued)*

Q: *How do you deal with stage parents?*

A: We try to explain about union houses and the rules governing the production, and that an infraction of a rule could cause the show to close. We try also to explain how dangerous it can be backstage with huge sets being moved around in the dark. In Washington, we have this misunderstanding often with young ballet dancers' parents who are used to their children performing in nonunion houses.

Q: *How can child performers stay children in the midst of an adult-business enterprise?*

A: By continuing to attend school where possible or keep up their lessons with the company tutor. They need to stay in touch with their school friends, or form friendships with other child performers or children whose parent(s) are in the business.

But other child performers had to learn the hard way to follow the rules. In *Mary Poppins*, one of the girls decided to cut her long blond hair just before rehearsals. When you've signed a contract for a show, it usually states you can't do anything to change your appearance, at least not without permission.

Because she looked very different from before, she had to wear a wig for performances. At first, she thought it was cool to have this new addition to her wardrobe. But the novelty wore off when she had to report to the theater half an hour earlier than before to get the wig styled properly before each show. The wig could also get uncomfortable—it made her head itch. She learned not to change her looks on a whim. Similarly, avoid tattoos and piercings! As an actor, you need to be able to transform yourself into any character you're hired to play—and not every character you audition for will have the same piercings and tattoos you do.

As a general rule, it's a good to have your hair look like it does in your headshot. It's less confusing for casting directors. Another general rule: It's better to have longer rather than very short hair, since it's easier to cut your hair to fit a part than to ask casting directors to imagine you with a wig or with grown-out hair.

With Katherine Doherty and Music Supervisor David Caddick at the edge of the orchestra pit, learning how to get an important cue from music director and conductor Brad Haak in "It's a Jolly Holiday with Mary" in *Mary Poppins* on Broadway.

I have learned that hair is often a big issue for both actors and stage management. In *The Little Mermaid*, when I played Flounder, for several days I thought my hair would be dyed bright yellow with neon-blue extensions woven in. Instead they decided on a wig. The wig looked really cool and the audience loved it.

Sometimes you have to dye your hair to match or contrast with the hair of other actors. In *The Orphans' Home Cycle*, there were three actors, including me, playing the main character. The two other actors had red hair, so I had to get my hair dyed red for consistency. After the show closed, the theater paid to have my hair dyed back to my normal brown.

There are other lessons to learn about your appearance when you are auditioning or performing. If you need braces, try to get the invisible kind, which use clear plastic, rather than metal bands. When I was younger, my teeth were slightly crooked. My orthodontist was able to fix my teeth with Invisalign, a system that uses clear plastic removable trays, kind of like mouthguards, rather than braces. They corrected the problem, and didn't cost me any lost parts, because I could take them out when performing or auditioning.

As a performer, you have to learn to avoid sunburns at all costs. When you are filming, your skin tone needs to be the same every day. Even in the theater, the makeup crew does not like it if you show up with a sunburn. When I went to the beach as a kid, I was covered in sunblock from

Working outside on the last day of "school" on the *Beauty and the Beast* tour, in sunny Jacksonville, FL. My awesome teacher and wrangler, Anne Marie Hurlbut, insisted I put a towel over my head (plus sunscreen!) so that I didn't get a sunburn. It was really fun to have class by the pool instead of inside. Even better to know summer vacation was starting the next day and I was already in Florida!

Theater Rules That I've Learned

Some of the rules of the theater are *rules*, some are customs, and some are just good sense.

- All members of the crew dress in black, so if they have to go across the stage, they can.

- Everyone calls Shakespeare's *Macbeth* "the Scottish play" and no one ever says the real title in the theater. It's no joke. Theater people are very superstitious about this. If you say the *M*-word in the theater, you'll be sent outside to run around the building three times to get rid of the bad luck that supposedly has come to productions of the play. Accidents and even deaths during runs of *Macbeth* are blamed on Shakespeare supposedly using real witches' spells, which then angered the witches and cursed the play.

- Don't play with Sharpies (which are lying around because you use them to sign autographs and the crew uses them to label equipment) or eat Skittles or M&M's when you're in costume. They can permanently color your clothes and dye your mouth.

- Don't touch anything backstage. Almost everything is breakable and needs to stay exactly where it is.

- Don't sit on anything backstage, including a chair, unless you are told by your wrangler or stage manager to sit there.

head to toe. When I am in a show, I almost always wear hats when I go out in the sun.

Through trial and error, I've also learned what type of work clothes are best for a performer. I usually wear cargo pants every day, simply because the pockets are so useful. I throw my wallet, subway pass, a flashlight, and an energy bar into them. For auditions, I always wear clothes that are appropriate for the role I'm trying out for. In New York, I learned about clothing stores' sample sales, which are good places to buy good-quality clothes inexpensively. I interned at one New York fashion house called Rag & Bone during Fashion Week. I was told to report at nine a.m. to the company's offices, which are in a cool building in the Meatpacking District. When I arrived, the fashion director yelled at me, "You're [expletive deleted] late!" He thought I was one of the models for the runway, which was a nice compliment. I got to run all over the city picking up buttons, fabrics, and Diet Cokes with caffeine for the staff.

The fashion director noticed the parachute-cord bracelets I make, which I was wearing that day. He had me make bracelets for the Rag & Bone models to wear on the runway—each model wore six bracelets. I quickly taught the other interns how to make them so we'd have enough for the show.

But I know better than to wear my parachute-cord bracelets for auditions, unless I think the character would normally be wearing street-style jewelry. It's also best to take hats and bling off when you step into an audition room.

While I was learning the importance of appearance in the theater, I also started learning the history and superstitions of the people who work in entertainment. Actors, stagehands, costumers, and other theater people told me the stories and explained unusual practices to me.

First, theaters always keep what's called a ghost light on, even when everyone has left the building. It's a plain lightbulb housed in a wire cage on top of a tall base, which is always left standing alone at night after the show, or whenever the theater is not being used for rehearsals or performances. The ghost light is there for safety, so stagehands can find the light switches when they first enter the building and so the last people off the stage can see where they are exiting—and so no one falls off the stage in the dark!

How to *Not* Sneeze and Yawn Onstage

How do you not sneeze onstage? You take shallow breaths from your upper chest. In the opera *Idomeneo*, I had to play dead onstage, and sometimes I felt as if I would sneeze. I just stifled it. I've also heard that looking into a bright light will help stop a sneeze.

When you see someone in the front row yawn, you have to stifle your impulse to do the same. It's contagious, but you can learn to hide it.

But the stage story is that the light is there so the theater's ghosts—thought to be the spirits of deceased actors who performed in that theater—can perform at night. The ghost light is also supposed to keep the theater from going "dark"—theater slang for when a show has closed and the theater stands unused, empty of life. No one wants a theater to go dark (except for maintenance), so the ghost light shines to prevent that.

Actors also don't say "Good luck," because the words are considered *bad* luck. Instead, we say, "Break a leg!" (Although ballet and modern dancers never say that, for obvious reasons! Most dancers prefer a French expression—see page 136.) There are many explanations for the phrase, including an actor taking so many bows because an audience keeps clapping that the actor will be bending (or breaking) his legs. Another explanation is that the theater's karma gives you the opposite of what you ask for, so that if you wish for bad luck, you'll get a successful turn onstage rather than a broken leg.

In other languages, performers have other ways of wishing one another bad luck as a backward way of wishing good luck. In French, they

say "Merde!" (which means *Poop!*—as in "Slip and fall in a pile of ——!").
In Italian, they say, "In boca al lupo!" ("Into the mouth of the wolf!") And
in Germany, you spit three times over the other performers' shoulders to
scare away the devil. It's useful to know these customs for when you work
with European performers.

Another superstition, and one that has a more clear-cut origin, is the
practice of not whistling in a theater. In times past, stagehands were
often former sailors who used a code of whistle signals, the same signals
they had used onboard ship, to tell one another what ropes should be
pulled to fly sets in and out. If an actor whistled, it could confuse things
backstage, causing real problems. A set piece could come crashing down
on someone's head!

Other forbidden behavior is often learned the hard way. For
example, never eat anything that might upset your stomach before a
show—or before a rehearsal, for that matter. When I was appearing in
Mary Poppins, the crew gave us candy before the show on Halloween.
Our child wrangler took all the kids on a little "trick-or-treat" run
throughout the backstage of the theater. One of the boys ate a lot of the
crew's gifts and complained of a stomachache before he went on. You
guessed it. He threw up onstage. Luckily, he did it behind a drop screen,
so the audience didn't see. It turned out he was allergic to apples and he
had eaten a caramel apple.

The stage manager immediately had to substitute another boy for his
part. Under union rules, any cast change must be announced over the
public-address system to the audience. Show managers really hate to do
that because it wrecks the magic of the moment and can throw off the
audience and the cast. From then on, before Halloween shows, the kids
got quarters and dollars from the crew instead of candy.

Sometimes, you have to learn to improvise onstage when things go
wrong. In one scene in *Mary Poppins*, the two kids run upstairs into the
elaborately furnished stage nursery while the lower floors of their house
slide toward the back of the stage. The nursery is then supposed to be
lowered three and a half stories until it reaches the deck, or stage floor.
As a precaution, a stage manager hides in the closet of the nursery with a
headset on to watch over the child actors on the set.

On our opening preview performance, we ran into the nursery. The

My Weirdest Makeup

In Mozart's opera *Idomeneo* at the Kennedy Center, in Washington, DC, I played the part of a dead young boy. I wore a flesh-toned Speedo bathing suit with fabric seaweed sewn on it. I'd lie down and the makeup folks would put "blood" (corn syrup mixed with red dye) on their hands and smear it on me. I was onstage like that for ten minutes, playing dead, before I was carried off.

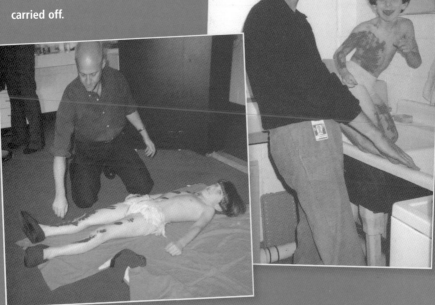

I wore slippers backstage to keep warm while the makeup crew painted my body with stage blood for Mozart's *Idomeneo*. They had to put a tarp under me to keep the floor clean. I was interviewed for a newspaper article while playing this role. The journalist asked if I didn't get cold running around backstage with almost no clothes on, smeared with "blood." I said I didn't mind because I am half English. Like my dad, I have a stiff upper lip! I had to stand in a backstage sink and have my stage blood washed off me after the show. It was a fun part, but the water was *cold*!

house moved back, the nursery roof rose, but the nursery just stood there. It felt like forever. The stage manager in the closet talked back and forth with the crew. Finally, the curtain went down and an announcement was made: "Ladies and gentlemen, we're having technical difficulties." It turned out the brake fluid in the apparatus had overheated, which could have affected the nursery's descent, but luckily there was a fail-safe maneuver that stopped things. Tom Schumacher, president of Disney Theatrical Group, came onstage and told jokes to the audience. About seven minutes later, everything was fixed and the show resumed.

Another time, the house came off its track as it was moving backward. During these moments, the crew is a like a flock of magic fairies. They use muscle and manpower to fix things fast. In this case, the crew pushed and tried to realign the house, but nothing worked. The house had to stay at the back of the stage throughout the rest of the show, but other than some changes to the lighting, the show went on without a hitch.

In *Chitty Chitty Bang Bang*, we were working with the most expensive stage prop ever made—the flying car. It's in the Guinness Book of World Records! It was an amazing piece of machinery, but on a few occasions, it did break down during a show. All of us would go to the front of the stage and stall, singing songs and asking who in the audience had their birthday that day. One time, we improvised a skit. One actor, Marc Kudisch, who played the baron of Vulgaria, took my shoe as I was sitting on the edge of the stage, trying to mock drag me into the orchestra pit. We did anything to keep the audience's spirits high. Once we were improvising gags for a full forty-five minutes.

Another stage prop, the tea cart in *Beauty and the Beast*, caused daily problems for me. My character, Chip, spends most of his time in the cart, with his head popping out of the top, with a large foam teacup framing my face. I had the reverse problem of most kids who played Chip—I was too small for the cart. In order to move my head around and open my jaw to talk and sing, it worked best if I stood as tall as possible. So I stood on my toes. I didn't think about it much until after my last show on tour. I was given my "blacks," the black clothes I wore inside the tea cart. It wasn't until then that I noticed I had worn a hole on the tips of both of my black shoes from standing on my toes in the cart for seven months. Maybe *that's* why my ballet teacher said I have a good pointe!

My Backstage "Home"

Unless your name is above the title, you'll share your dressing room with other actors. The girls share one and the boys another. Broadway theaters are pretty old and the dressing rooms have been home to hundreds of actors.

I always have a chair, a small patch of counter space, and usually a mirror with lights around it. I put my backpack under my counter, out of the way. Everyone personalizes their space with break-a-leg cards, opening-night wishes, and photos. At Christmas, we do Secret Santa. Your Santa might string lights around your mirror and hang up a stocking.

Backstage, in corridors, you'll see the dressers repairing costumes and the crew reading, doing crossword puzzles, or studying. Some actors make jewelry or knit sweaters. It's cramped—like being on a submarine! The show is piped into every dressing room, so that's your focus—listening closely for your warning cues.

One time, I had to deal with being hurt (by accident) on the stage. In the last scene of *A Christmas Carol*, my stage father, Bob Cratchit, carried me on his shoulders through a doorway onstage. He forgot to duck and my forehead smacked into the doorframe, knocking the wind out of me. Fortunately, he had a good grip on my legs and I didn't fall off. Everyone onstage was a bit shocked, but tried to act normal. My stage father propped me up with my crutch in time for my next line. After I said the last line of the show, "God bless us every one," the curtain went down and the whole cast cheered. I wore the huge bump on my head as a badge of honor.

The Washington, DC, cast of *A Christmas Carol* also had to deal with an unexpected visitor onstage: a rat! During the Christmas party dance scene, Mrs. Fezziwig has some lines about the "good cheer of the season," at which point a rat scurried out onstage. It went straight under Mrs. Fezziwig's floor-length skirt. She didn't see it, but it was at eye level for most of the audience, who murmured and chuckled. Mrs. Fezziwig thought she was really connecting with the audience and gave even more energy to her performance. As if on cue, the rat ran off and exited stage left. He never even came back for a bow.

Some improvisations onstage are necessary because an actor screws up. It happened to me in *To Kill a Mockingbird*, and believe me, I never made the mistake again. In one scene, my character, Jem, catches his overalls on a fence as he's running offstage to spy on his neighbor, Boo Radley. When Jem returns to the stage, he's wearing just his 1930s boxer briefs.

At one special school matinee, I forgot to put on the costume boxers and only wore my regular underwear. It wasn't until I was offstage and taking off my overalls in the dark wings that I realized I didn't have on the costume boxers. All I could do was run back onstage in my regular tighty whities and continue with the scene. Some of the kids in the audience shrieked and laughed. I never forgot the boxers again.

With Olivia Scott (as Scout) in *To Kill a Mockingbird*—wearing my infamous 1930s undies. . . .

Performers Live in a Different World

When you are performing full-time, your life becomes different from the lives of your neighborhood and school friends. Whether you're on tour for months or simply out of town in a production, you're going to miss out on birthdays, sleepovers, sports events, and family get-togethers.

Technology has made it easier to stay in touch. My father read me all the Harry Potter books each night—by telephone. That was our special

In the Hilton hotel in Hartford, CT, while on the road for *Beauty and the Beast*, listening to my dad read the latest installment of Harry Potter. I have my stuffed animals ready for bed—the Beast, Lumière the candlestick, Cogsworth the clock—all characters in the show. Over the years when I was touring continually, Dad also read me the complete Sherlock Holmes novels and short stories by Sir Arthur Conan Doyle—over the phone. Truly, heroic bedtime-story duty.

One of the best things about the *Beauty and the Beast* tour was that my older sister, Charly, got to pinch-hit in the merchandise department as her summer job. They needed extra help and she turned out to kill as a saleswoman! While working on the tour, Charly caught the travel bug. After she finished college, she got a great job with an international and educational travel company. It was so much fun getting to travel together. That's Charly (*left*) with me and Charly's merchandising boss, Dominique Hogue.

time, every night. It took months and months. It was our time to connect.

My older sister, Charly, stays in touch with me by Skype, e-mail, and the phone. One of the best breaks I got while on tour with *Beauty and the Beast* was when Charly got to join us for the summer, selling show merchandise. That was so much fun, having her with my mom and me as we explored new cities.

I missed our dog so much that my family got me a pet mouse, Scabbers, when my mom and I lived in a New York City apartment. He was the smartest

mouse. He sat on my shoulder as I walked and would fall asleep on my chest when I was doing my homework.

9

Protecting Yourself

Racing up the stairs to the nursery in *Mary Poppins*. During our first preview on Broadway, this huge piece of scenery failed to lower to the stage as it was supposed to. From a young age, I had to learn how to work around big pieces of machinery. Everything is so fast-paced backstage, you can definitely get hurt—or hurt someone else—and cause all kinds of problems by getting in the way. The crew works hard to make everything fail-safe, but things sometimes go wrong, especially with motorized or automated elements. Safety always comes first!

Being a performer is so, well, entertaining that you can forget it is a craft and a profession. Safety is key—personally and financially. There are national laws that protect you on the job and some state laws that require that part of your earnings be put aside in a trust fund. I've also learned a lot about protecting my voice and my stamina and how to work around adults.

Your young age is an advantage, but you also have to grow up from "cute" to young adult. I had to deal with my voice changing and to prepare for young-adult roles in dramas.

When you're working onstage, or on a movie set, at a photo shoot, or in a recording studio, you need to stay away from equipment and cables on the floor. Resist your natural curiosity to turn knobs or touch

I do love to goof around a little bit backstage, but really, no one at the Kennedy Center was going to turn on the dryer while I was in it! I did learn early how important it is to stay close by the child wrangler for safety. I snuck in the dryer just long enough to have my picture taken.

things. There's so much work behind the scenes, with the costumes, set, automation, and sound. It's a very regulated environment, with trained professionals handling things. Your job is to not get in the way.

People organizing the play, movie, photo shoot, or recordings are very busy, and wasted time costs them money. Equipment is expensive and may be rented for just a few hours or days. The message my child wranglers and parents drilled into me was that if we would always stick close to them, we'd all be safe. Paying attention in rehearsals, especially technical rehearsals, is important.

Getting a show "up" or "up on its feet" usually follows a routine. You begin your work in rehearsal studios, which in New York are located all over the Theater District. Many outsiders think actors spend all their rehearsal time on the theater's stage. In fact, this is impossible most of the time, because another show may be playing in your theater while yours is in rehearsal, or the crew for your show may be building the sets onstage. And most older theaters don't have any rehearsal space on-site. So you work in rental studios, which usually are big white rooms, often with wall-to-wall mirrors and sprung wooden floors—floors that can absorb movement because they're backed with foam or rubber or built on a bouncy lattice of wooden crosspieces underneath.

Rehearsals are specialized. One room might have the choreographer working with dancers on a big number. In another room, the director might be working with a few actors. In a third room, the music director could be going over a big solo with a performer. Rehearsals take a lot of effort and there's a lot of repetition. You can spend a lot of time before it's your turn to practice.

After several weeks, the actors have memorized the songs and the lines and are off book, the dances have been choreographed and learned, and everyone knows their basic blocking. The whole operation then moves to the theater for "tech," or technical rehearsals. Things are very different once you get onstage. Maybe there's a piece of set in your way now, or you're not used to working on a raked (slanted) stage. Sound and lights are added, and you have to remember sound and visual cues, which you didn't have in rehearsal.

Tech can seem to go on forever. The actors sit around in the audience area in the darkened theater, waiting to go on. Some actors take naps,

A Child Wrangler Speaks

Christina Huschle worked as a child wrangler on Broadway for several years, including a stint on *Mary Poppins*, where she and I first met. Here are some of her thoughts on working with me and other child performers.

Q: *How do kids get their cues? Handle their costumes?*

A: Most of my experience comes from a show in which the children were principal actors. Therefore, they received intense rehearsal periods with the director and choreographer.

It is expected that the child will arrive on his/her first day of rehearsal "off book" [having memorized all of his or her lines and cue lines]. During rehearsal, the director/choreographer/stage manager teaches them the blocking and choreography. As the wrangler, I watched to make sure the child was "getting it" and helped reiterate the rules of safe conduct backstage.

The costumes in a Broadway show are covered by the child's dresser. The children are given strict instructions about how to care for the costume while wearing it. Normal wear and tear is expected, but it is driven home that the expensive costumes are not theirs and [that] they must treat them with respect. Only in special circumstances, such as onstage changing of costumes, are the children allowed to handle the costumes on their own.

Q: *What is the toughest part of your job as a wrangler?*

A: It is managing disappointment. An actor's life is full of disappointments: losing the part to another person, losing a job because you no longer fit the costume, etc. But being disappointed is something adults try to shield children from—and you can't in this business. For every opening night, there is a closing night.

Wranglers, like parents, are front-row center for the child's disappointment. Knowing these early disappointments are learning tools doesn't help when a kid's eyes fill with tears. I always tried to keep a stiff upper lip and remind the child that the audience doesn't need to know they are disappointed or sad and to give the best show he/she can. On final performances, I tended to have "the show must go on" speeches ready in case a child wanted to break down when the show needed him to keep it up. I may have seemed heartless in the moment, but I was also making sure that the child had a great final show.

Q: *How did you get into this business?*

A: My best friend's older sister from back home was the wrangler on another show, and she gave me a substitute position when I moved to New York City. I absolutely loved it. The job melded two of my skills: being good with kids and the theater. When the opportunity to do it as my real job presented itself, I jumped at the chance. I was on Broadway for five and a half years and wrangled thirty-six kids before moving on.

Q: *What attributes, in Henry and others, make the experience go smoothly?*

A: As a wrangler, I found that the kids most suited for working at a young age are mature for their age, able to go with the flow and entertain themselves. (Notice I didn't mention that they have to be talented!) One of the first things I noticed about Henry was that he didn't need me. Not that he wasn't friendly or open to having me around, but that he was self-sufficient.

While some of the other kids needed my attention and assistance to get through their day, Henry was happy to quietly study his lines or have

Continues . . .

a conversation with one of the adults or just basically chill out while we waited for our turn to rehearse.

Sometimes there would be children whose parents did everything for them: tie shoes, button coats, and remind them to drink water. As a wrangler, my philosophy was, if you are capable of performing for three hours in front of an audience, you can blow your nose without help. I had to break in many a child in my time, but they always left the show ready to take on the world.

Q: *What advice do you give young performers?*

A: I gave the kids lectures—lectures upon lectures about safety. Lectures they could recite back to me. They loved to hear horror stories of children past— the kid who threw up onstage, the time the kid lost the tooth in the middle of this song, etc. From those stories, the kids had basic ideas of what to do when something unexpected happened.

Q: *How should a young girl or boy prepare for stints in the theater?*

A: Having talent and abilities is a given. The skills and attributes that are most important for a working child have absolutely nothing to do with talent. A child should love to work hard at something they love. If they get bored easily, even with something they enjoy, how will they get through a four-hour rehearsal, let alone four shows a week? A child should be patient and happy to wait around quietly. A child should be flexible and open to change. Basically, the child should be mature enough to know that, once at the theater, the whole world doesn't revolve around them.

Q: *What hazards should they watch out for?*

A: There are the obvious physical hazards of being onstage with moving set pieces. Show kids also are part of an adult world, and wranglers, while they try, can't be everywhere. But the biggest hazard is the inherent competitiveness of acting. There are only so many roles for children in this business. While it is hard to see children upset about growing older, it is harder to explain why other kids are mean or jealous just because of a part or an opportunity.

Q: *How do you deal with stage parents?*

A: Parents can help make the job of wrangler easier and blissful, or they can completely ruin a kid. I kept parents abreast of the things they needed to know (rehearsal times, the need for food, and if the child was looking sick) and kept them out of the day-to-day of being in the dressing room (little arguments, problems I could handle).

Q: *How can child performers stay children in the midst of an adult-business enterprise?*

A: The best way for a child to remain a child while being a child actor is to hang out with regular kids. Stay on a soccer team or in the school choir; have sleepovers with kids from school when shows end. Don't let the parent become the child's only friend. The child will start to emulate the parents/caregiver if he spends all of his time with adults. In my experience, the kids who had friends outside of the business were the happiest and remained regular kids themselves.

Continues . . .

A Child Wrangler Speaks (continued)

Q: *You would take the children performing in* Mary Poppins *to lunch in a nearby park during rehearsals. Can you tell us about that and several other activities that became theater traditions?*

A: The famous Poppins Park was the McCaffrey Playground on West Forty-Third Street between Eighth and Ninth Avenues. Another tradition began when one of the original little girls wanted to decorate the clock I bought for the floor when we first moved into the theater in October 2006. We cut all of the children's headshots out of the *Playbill* and put them on numbers on the clock. When it was time for the first children to leave, she asked me what I was going to do with her picture on the clock. I had no idea.

So I invented the Hall of Fame. I wrote up a little good-bye and asked the two children who were leaving if they would read it out loud to each other on their last performance. I thought maybe involving the actress who played Mary Poppins might be a nice touch. She agreed and brought her parrot umbrella. We invited a few people to come watch and the rest is history. For the last five and a half years, the Hall of Fame Ceremony is the one thing a departing young actor can look forward to—the moment when they are special and important, and they know they are leaving their mark for the future children to see. Everyone who can comes to cheer the child on and we all have a good cry before they get out in front of the audience.

Also, the "Happy Trails" song from Roy Rogers's show is sung whenever a cast member leaves a show. It is different for everyone, but at *Mary Poppins* we sing it after the curtain call. Everyone gets in a big circle and sings the song at the top of their lungs. The children absolutely live for "Happy Trails" because it's so emotional and dramatic. When a child is the one leaving, there are many tears and usually a little speech. The one thing almost every child has ever said is that he will miss being part of the family of the show. They will miss being involved in something so magical.

but I can't, because I'll feel too groggy when I wake up. Every two hours, we get a fifteen-minute break, announced by the stage manager.

During tech, the producers sometimes have dinner brought in and tables with food set up in the greenroom. The etiquette for the actors is first come, first served, and there's always a stampede for the food. The crew always gets served second, as their break starts after the actors'. This is one reason why there's sometimes a little bit of antagonism between crew and performers and why you want to be a friend to all.

I took these pictures myself. Every theater has its own rules for backstage safety. Some of them are a little more offbeat than others. . . .

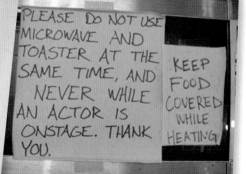

You learn in tech just how much work is involved in entertainment. There's always a time in tech where everything seems to be going wrong. Light cues won't work or the automation of some scenic element fails. This is normal, a result of so many components of the show being linked together for the first time. You will learn a new skill—patience—during tech.

The most fun I had in tech was rehearsing the dream sequence in *Chitty Chitty Bang Bang*, in which I fly over the stage. Many shows use a flying system provided by a company called Flying by Foy, whose employees work with the actors. I told the Flying by Foy guy that I wanted to try a flip in the air. He told me he'd rig me safely, let me do the flip, and then ask the director if it could be included. I did the flip and it got put in the show. That was so exciting to perform. Aerial work does make you feel like a bird.

Safeguard Your Health

Protecting kids onstage is everyone's business. But protecting your body from illness is your concern. Not getting sick is a big part of being a performer. Don't whine about wanting to go on sleepovers when you're in a show. You know you'll stay up most of the night goofing off with your friends and will be too dead tired to perform well the next day. If you get sick, you're letting down the cast and crew.

In the winter, I take vitamin C and echinacea every day, use a humidifier, and wash my hands a lot. On my rest days, when I don't have a performance, I barely talk all day. If my throat feels weird, I gargle with warm water and salt.

I try to avoid junk food and have learned to eat many more vegetables (Brussels sprouts, broccoli, and green beans, especially). But I still have a sweet tooth.

I added certain classes to my day to build up my strength. Ballet classes in pointe work, which I took at age fourteen, really strengthened my ankles. (Usually only girls and women perform in pointe shoes, but some boys and men do study pointe technique at some, well, *point* in their training, and it helps a lot.) I needed more upper-body strength

Even though few men ever perform on pointe, toe shoes are amazing for developing strong feet and ankles and good balance. Here one of my instructors, Yuka Kawazu, gives me a few pointe-ers at a studio in New York City where many teachers and choreographers rent studios by the hour. You must be careful not to start pointe work too young because of the pressure it puts on your foot bones. I'm lucky that Yuka taught a class with guys in it. When I was 6, I wanted tap lessons, but ended up in tae kwon do instead because there weren't any dance classes for boys. For guys, it is also important to learn dance moves such as lifts and other partnering techniques that aren't covered in normal ballet classes.

My Offstage Fun in New York City

You could never live long enough to enjoy everything the Big Apple has to offer!

- Attending a Broadway Show League softball game at one of the Heckscher Ballfields in Central Park. Games are on Thursdays at 11:30 a.m. from late April through June. Broadway and Off-Broadway shows have teams, but cast members have to be sixteen to participate.

- Walking the High Line, a relatively new urban park built on an old elevated railway. It stretches from Gansevoort Street in the West Village all the way up to West Thirtieth Street between Tenth and Eleventh Avenues, with views of the Hudson River. (Eventually, the park will be extended to Thirty-Fourth Street.)

- Exploring Riverside Park and Pier 86 near West Forty-Sixth Street. The pier is home to the Intrepid Sea, Air & Space Museum. In the summer there is free fishing with free rods and bait on the pier. There's also free kayaking and a water fountain to run through, plus a bike trail along the Hudson River that goes past both locales.

- Enjoying Bryant Park at Forty-Second Street and Sixth Avenue. There is free ice-skating in the winter and a free Monday night film festival in the summer. Both are popular, so get to the park early to secure a good space for your blanket. There also is a small merry-go-round and an outdoor library.

- Visiting the Children's Zoo, near Fifth Avenue and Sixty-Sixth Street, inside the Central Park Zoo. Here you can pet and feed goats, sheep, cows, pigs, and llamas in the middle of the city. The zoo has a great seal pool and a refrigerated penguin house.

- Experiencing Chelsea Piers, at Pier 60, Nineteenth Street and the Hudson River. The complex offers many sports and activities, including parkour/free running, gymnastics, and rock climbing. There's also a golf driving range overlooking the river. Note to actors: The *Law & Order* auditions are held here!

Safeguarding your *mental* health includes taking time to relax and have fun. Rowing in Central Park is a lovely way to while away an afternoon. The park is the best playground for kids. Its zoo is terrific and there's ice-skating all winter long. Nearly every sport imaginable is being played by someone in the park whenever you visit. I also like going to the park to see the leaves turning colors in the fall and to go sledding when it snows.

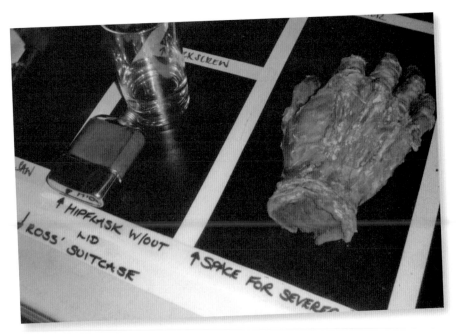

Here, a bloody hand from the Scottish play (as Shakespeare's *Macbeth* is always called in the theater) on the prop table. If a show has props—and most do—they are laid out like this on long tables backstage, with each prop in its own labeled spot outlined in white tape. Never mess around with the props! You don't want the crew to take their revenge on you as someone did on this poor guy.

to improve in gymnastics. I worked at it and now can do front and back handsprings, roundoffs, and back tucks.

But as every actor knows, your voice is your biggest concern. Even if you're not singing, your work puts big demands on your throat. Voice-over sessions for movies can last two to four hours. That's a lot of enthusiastic talking! It takes about eight sessions to do a whole movie.

Once, in a recording studio, I had to repeat a line thirty times to say it "perfectly." That's part of the gig. Having to record many takes happens more with commercials, because there may be, for example, a medical term you don't know in the script, and it may take several tries to get the pronunciation and intonation right.

For boy actors, you have to deal with your voice changing. I found out what happens when your voice cracks before a packed house on Broadway.

As the character of Michael Banks in *Mary Poppins*, I was on the stage, singing out our attic bedroom window. My lyric was, "I just feel as if I'm dreaming, / So much fun in just one day!" They were exactly the beautiful solo high notes you dream about singing—until your voice cracks for the first time on the very highest note.

My voice had felt slightly funny for about a month. I had worked at keeping it in line, but this time my voice had its own idea. I caught the eye of Brad Haak, who was conducting the orchestra. With baton in hand he paused for a slight second, grimaced with one raised eyebrow, and then smiled.

I knew at that moment, it was over. I was fifteen and had been anticipating this for years. My voice was off by just a fraction, but that's all it takes. It was a bittersweet moment—the end to all the singing parts I had landed and my hopes for the ones I hadn't gotten yet, for a while at least.

Because I was growing taller, I had known my days on *Mary Poppins* were numbered. I had already been cast in the upcoming Broadway production of *Macbeth*, a straight play with no singing. Like many people in the theater, I was working two jobs at once, rehearsing for *Macbeth* and performing and standing by in *Mary Poppins*. (I performed the role three times a week and was the standby for two other shows.)

Before the next *Mary Poppins* performance, I had "the talk" with stage management about my voice. Everyone was very supportive and I still performed a few more times. But we agreed on a date for me to leave. Before my last show, Brad said at half hour to curtain, "You are going to hate me for this, but tonight we're changing a few of your notes." We joked around and he helped me through it. After more than a year and a half of shows, I sang different, lower notes instead of some of the highest ones in the songs for my last performance. A few years later I ran into another former Michael Banks who had followed me at some point and had left the show for the same reason. It turns out those new lower notes are now called "the Henry notes."

Others helped me in the transition from child to young-adult roles. The Broadway casting agent Bernard Telsey believed in my ability to move from child parts in musicals to young-adult roles in straight plays. That put me on my way.

My father in *To Kill a Mockingbird* was the actor Matthew Modine, who is best known for his film roles. He showed me acting techniques and how to come alive before a camera. A crew filmed the show for the "B-roll," which is footage used for advertising and public relations. Matthew understood the leap I was making and helped me develop more adult acting skills.

Safeguard Your Finances

Protecting your money is your parents' concern until you get older, but you should know that laws in California and New York require employers to put aside 15 percent of your income in a trust fund until you are eighteen. In New York, the law requiring this is the New York Child Performer Education and Trust Act of 2003. It also requires that child performers meet certain rules about their education. In California, it's called the Coogan Law, and Louisiana and New Mexico have adopted it too. The law was named after the child actor Jackie Coogan, who was discovered by Charlie Chaplin in 1919 and made famous in his 1921 movie *The Kid*. After Coogan turned twenty-one, he found out that the money he had earned from films and merchandise with his likeness on it was all gone. He had to sue his own mother and his former manager.

Before a state labor department gives you a work permit, you must show that your parents or guardians have set up a trust account for you. Your parents or guardians are further required to give the trust account number to any employers before you start work.

Safeguard Your Mental Health

You can get caught up in the time pressures of the entertainment world as well. Protecting your happiness, therefore, is another important job. I tell myself to enjoy every bit of my time on- and offstage, because I'll only be young once.

My dad and I dressed up for the Helen Hayes Awards at the Kennedy Center—Washington's version of the Tony Awards. My family comes to all my openings and other theater events. We keep up by Skype, telephone, text—it's easy to keep in touch with modern technology.

You also don't want your family's entire life to revolve around your work schedule. Your sisters and brothers will get very tired of too much attention going your way.

We always tried to plan ahead and have family days of fun and exploration. New York is a great city for free outdoor activities. I spend so much time inside when I'm in theater shows and productions that you can pretty much bet I'm outdoors on my days off.

10

Swing, Cover, Understudy— The Show Must Go On

Ellen Marlow and I, who performed together in *Chitty Chitty Bang Bang*, visiting the dogs who performed in the show. There were seven performing dogs, and one *understudy*! All of the actors loved to pet the dogs, who were trained by Bill Berloni, the top animal trainer on Broadway. He trains cats, birds, dogs, and even rats for the stage. He rescues his dogs from animal shelters. There was one scene in which the dogs rush into the sweets factory. One night a dog ran out and then kept running off the stage and into the orchestra pit! Fortunately for everyone, there was a safety net over the pit and no one was hurt. Bill took the dog to the vet and it turned out the dog needed a cataract operation. His understudy stepped in and played the part until the lead dog recovered from the surgery—just like human performers. During *Chitty* the whole cast fell in love with our furry cast mates. After the show closed a few of the cast members adopted some of their canine friends. The rest went to live the life of an actor between jobs, on the ninety acres where Bill lives in Haddam, CT, with twenty-six working and retired show dogs.

Flexibility is essential to any performer's life. My flexibility was tested to the max when I worked as an understudy on Broadway—one of the hardest jobs I've ever had. The positive side was that learning how to handle this behind-the-scenes role was a tremendous learning experience.

There are different ways of becoming an understudy. You can be cast in the ensemble, or have some other part in a show, and also be cast as an understudy for a leading part. So, if you're a dancing saltshaker in *Beauty and the Beast*, you might also be a townsperson and a wolf in other scenes. These parts are called part of your "track." On top of that, you could be cast as an understudy for the Beast. So if the actor who plays the Beast gets sick or goes on vacation, you could be asked by stage management to go on. So who goes on for your parts?

That actor is called the *swing*. That actor is the understudy for the understudy. Swings wait backstage, prepared to go on for multiple parts at a moment's notice. I have the utmost respect for swings. They have all of the work and none of the glory. It's a very complicated job that most audience members don't even know exists.

Another type of understudy is a *standby*. A standby literally waits backstage in case the actor who plays that character can't go on because they get sick or injured in the show. Standbys usually don't do anything else in the show. It is a very hard job to wait backstage, maybe for months at a time, never knowing if you will ever go onstage at all.

My friend Rozi Baker was the standby for Young Bonnie in the Broadway musical *Bonnie & Clyde*. She had previously played three roles in *Shrek, the Musical* and also starred as Jane Banks in *Mary Poppins*, both on Broadway. She is a wonderful performer and singer. She never got to perform her part as Young Bonnie, but she was excited to be part of the original cast of that terrific show.

Understudies are also called *covers*, and sometimes there can be as many as three covers for a lead role.

In my only experience as an understudy, there was much I didn't know at first. For example, who would guess that understudies often are paid more than actors in onstage roles? One reason is that one understudy may cover several lead roles. That's a lot more memorization—more blocking, more dance steps, and more costume changes to master.

The maximum number of roles one actor can understudy is five! On Broadway, actors are paid at least $40 a week more for each additional

Stage Shorthand

Actors often scribble a special code of initials in their scripts during rehearsals when they are blocking their movements. These initials are a sort of shorthand to note where you should stand, enter, or exit. For all rehearsals, bring a pencil with an eraser, as blocking often changes. Here are some common stage notations:

US—upstage (the area farthest from the audience)

CS—center stage

DS—downstage

L—left

R—right

X—cross

DR—downstage right

DL—downstage left

UR—upstage right

UL—upstage left

CL—center stage left

CR—center stage right

The terms *upstage* and *downstage* come from old-fashioned raked (sloping) stages, on which upstage really *is* higher than downstage. In most modern theaters, the stage is flat (even if some set elements built on the stage are raked) and the house (audience seating area) is raked, which is safer for the performers and allows everyone to see. *Stage right* and *stage left* are so called from the *performers'* point of view, facing the house.

role they understudy, which is added to the usual $1,703 per week an understudy receives as a Broadway minimum.

Another surprise to me was that understudies don't rehearse along with the onstage actors before the opening. Understudies' rehearsals usu-ally come several weeks later, once the show is up and running. This is why it's such a heart-stopping moment when an understudy is asked to go on, especially early in a show's run. They may not be totally prepared and they certainly haven't worked out a comfortable relationship with the main cast.

Before they have formal rehearsals, understudies memorize the lines and watch the main cast rehearse. When they do rehearse, understudies work only with stage management and other understudies, not the principal actors.

There is also what is called a *put-in rehearsal*, when you take over a part in a show that's already running. The whole cast assembles and performs the scenes that you are in. This happened to me in *Beauty and the Beast*. The show had been running longer than I had been alive, so I was a *replacement*. A replacement is any actor taking over a part who was not in the show when it opened.

Child roles can be double or triple cast because of work rules that dictate how many days and hours children can work. Sometimes the part is cast with one principal, plus a standby, who is not scheduled to go on. Or the part may be cast with a principal and an ensemble member who plays the part regularly, maybe once a week during a matinee. Sometimes the part is double cast and both principals share the role equally, as I did playing Chip in *Beauty and the Beast*. For triple casting, one child actor is on, one stands by, and one has a day off. This is the arrangement that was used for *Mary Poppins* and *Billy Elliot*.

But there are other variations. When I was cast as Jeremy Potts in *Chitty Chitty Bang Bang*, I assumed I was cast with another boy who would alternate with me. But I later found out I was the only Jeremy and had three understudies in the ensemble. When I was in *Macbeth*, there were two boy parts and three actors hired. The two other boys each played only one character. I played both characters and we all played the same number of shows.

Child actors in the theater usually aren't famous, so there's less disappointment from the audience if a child understudy goes on. Even without dealing with audience disappointment, most understudies still have to live with the tension of going onstage with little notice, and saying the star's words or singing their songs.

Having been both a lead and an understudy, I know that other cast members are truly appreciative of an understudy's being able to jump

Lots of theater people are clowns at heart, so there can be a little bit of mayhem backstage and in the dressing rooms. Here, Aldrin Gonzalez, who played LeFou in *Beauty*, is showing off his strength by holding me upside down (some of his teeth are blacked-out because LeFou gets them knocked out when he's punched by Gaston). I've got my wig cap on, but no wig yet. If he had dropped me on my head, my standby would have had to go on. . . .

into a show with little notice. The audience may not see anything different in the production, but the rest of the cast knows how difficult it is to join a production that's already moving to its own rhythm.

It is a different experience being cast as an understudy. You don't get the preparation for the role that the other actors receive. Usually, you don't know when or if you are going on. You spend a lot of time preparing on your own and waiting for the call.

I was cast as an understudy in *13* on Broadway and only went onstage once. But it was a very useful experience because it gave me a new appreciation for all understudies. I know what it's like to want the part but be restricted to waiting in the wings.

The great thing about being an understudy is that you are fully part of the show. You are working, learning a new role, and making important contacts with other actors and staff members. Always use understudying as an opportunity to show others how professional your work ethic is. Also, you could end up taking over for the lead and becoming the star of the show. It happens: Many starring performers have started out as understudies.

This is the end of my big solo number in Disney's *The Little Mermaid* in Sacramento: "She's in love! She's in love! Ye-e-e-eah, yeah!"—but unfortunately not with Flounder (me). :-/

11

Some Drawbacks

Family meals go by the wayside when you're on the road as a child actor. My mom and I often cooked on a hot plate in our hotel room during *Beauty and the Beast*.

As fun filled and exciting as it can be to work as a performer, there are downsides. You get rejected at most auditions. Rehearsals can be difficult and waiting around can seem to last forever. Critics are mean. Shows close.

Knowing in advance some of the negatives can help you follow the great British wartime motto: Keep calm and carry on. That's what I try to do.

I learned that sometimes audiences disappoint you. Their cell phones ring. They're texting and we can see their phones lighting up their faces. Raúl Esparza, a major leading actor, stopped our show once when someone in the second row was reading a book.

Many actors dislike school matinees because some schoolkids are not respectful. They'll scream if something's scary or yell, "Oh no, she didn't!" when a character has a dramatic moment.

Childlike behavior by others can affect me backstage as well. If one kid actor in a show does something wrong, the child wrangler will usually punish the entire group of kids. Rooms will be put off-limits or freedoms will be restricted for everyone, because that's easier than devising a punishment for just one kid.

Stage fright, audition nerves, and "the actor's nightmare" all can be a part of your life. Actor Ewan McGregor described this basic actor's nightmare to *People* magazine this way: "You're about to go onstage, you can't find the script, you don't know what the play is, and you can't remember your lines." Almost every performer has had that bad dream. After I left *Beauty and the Beast* and *Mary Poppins*, I dreamed that stage management called at half hour before curtain and said all the kids were sick, could I just get to the theater and they'd have the costume ready?

The unexpected is a constant in the arts. You'll spend weeks rehearsing and feel good about your voice and your command of a role. Then you get into the actual theater and it's much harder to project. The chairs, the people in the audience, and the costumes just soak up the sound.

The script and choreography can change at any time, often at the last minute. Key people in the show can leave, get sick, or be replaced. You need to be prepared and organized to roll with the punches.

On your days off, you have to be more careful than most kids are. No loud talking. Sleepovers are a risk, so you have to say no to your friends

Crazy Facts About Broadway

Broadway is a beehive of activity, one big, giant melting pot. If you can't find it in NYC, you probably can't find it anywhere.

- Broadway began as a Native American trail. As a road, it is the oldest north–south main thoroughfare in New York City, dating back to the Dutch colony of New Amsterdam; the name Broadway is a literal translation of the old Dutch name, Breede weg.

- Broadway is the longest street in Manhattan. It starts at the southern tip of the island and keeps going 150 miles north, all the way to Albany, the state capital (though its name changes first to Highland Avenue and then to the Albany Post Road as it passes through the town of Sleepy Hollow).

- Theater people's "weekends" are Mondays, and we all work on almost all holidays.

- Church bells at Saint Malachy's Church on West Forty-Ninth Street play "There's No Business like Show Business" half an hour before showtimes.

- All theaters, and Saint Malachy's, dim their lights to honor a major performer or theater producer when he or she dies.

- The Theater District's other name, the Great White Way, came from a 1902 headline in the *New York Evening Telegram*. It read "Found on the Great White Way" because lightbulbs were new and theater marquees and billboards lit up the night.

sometimes. You have to watch out for sugar and mint—both are bad for your throat.

You also have to protect your heart from the sadness of show closings. When I left the touring show of *Beauty and the Beast*, I cried. I had to say good-bye to so many friends. But I was only ten. Since then, I've never cried when leaving a show. I realized that you still see many people from your past shows.

Of course, when I walk by the New Amsterdam Theatre now and see the *Mary Poppins* marquee, it hits me that others are playing Michael Banks now. But I can't play a nine-year-old forever. I played that part for a year and a half. You learn to move on with happiness for what was.

The business side of the industry is also a lot to learn for beginners. As one music blogger put it, "The wannabes have no idea how sophisticated the game is." A 2012 documentary, *The Hollywood Complex*, focused on a complex in Los Angeles that rents apartments to families of child actors who come during the five-month pilot season hoping to land a TV show. As Cleveland *Plain Dealer* newspaper writer Joanna Connors wrote when reviewing the film, the reality can be tough: "As the months go by without many successes, the kids' unflagging self-confidence, coupled with their almost total lack of self-awareness and industry savvy, is both breathtaking and a bit depressing." But if you're surrounded by a supportive family and teachers who give you realistic feedback, you can avoid setting yourself up for disappointment.

Living out of a suitcase—which is a way of life for many child actors—can make some kids homesick for their friends and life at home. My mom and I made every city an adventure, so living in hotel rooms became a big treat. We had a hot plate we brought with us to cook eggs, so we could stay in our pajamas for breakfast and not have to eat cold cereal every morning.

The show gives you a per diem amount for food, but sometimes you just don't feel like finding a restaurant for every meal. Sometimes it's hard to find any food at all. Once, our bus rolled into Asheville, NC, just before 10 p.m. The word went out that the only place open was an ice cream parlor that was closing in fifteen minutes. We all crowded inside and ordered banana splits for dinner! Sometimes, your hotel room will have a small kitchen. If we can, we shop at farmers' markets and stock up. We always pack family photos to put up in the room.

Room service is a big treat—and a *rare* treat. Here, pancakes—one of my favorites—in a hotel while on tour. Touring actors get into town at weird hours, so room service can be a lifesaver. But be careful to look at the prices on the menu!

As an actor, you almost always work every holiday, because that's when your audiences most want to see a show. I've worked so many Thanksgivings that we started our own family tradition around the Macy's parade, which is in the morning, rather than a dinner at night when I'm working. When we're all together in New York, my family usually views the parade from a friend's office just above the parade route. We have a party with friends, family, bagels—it's New Yawk, ya gotta have bagels!— and pumpkin pie. Then we go back to our apartment to relax for a few hours, eat an amazing takeout Thanksgiving dinner from the Amish market on Ninth Avenue, and watch the annual James Bond Marathon—my favorite!—on Spike TV. I loved working in *A Christmas Carol* over the holidays. It was a party every day onstage. Now when I go to holiday parties,

I can sing along to all the old-fashioned Christmas carols I learned while performing in the show.

When you are performing in a show, your internal clock runs differently from normal. After an evening show, your adrenaline is pounding through your bloodstream and your heart rate is up. You're ready to do something other than sleep. One time we went bowling at midnight. If it was the last night in a city, the other child actors and I could stay up and watch a movie in the hotel because we knew we could sleep the next day.

Jealousy also is a fact of life. There is such competition for parts that sometimes kids don't handle rejection very well.

It is always interesting to look at the sign-up sheets in auditions—to see who your competition is. But I'm lucky to have friends I can compete with and still stay friends with. You need to understand that casting directors are always looking for *the one* who is the right person for the role. If you don't get the part, it's rarely because you really messed up an audition. It could be because the director wanted someone of a different size or with a different look. They might be looking for a younger version of an actor who has already been cast who looks nothing like you. You're just out of luck then, but you never know until you try. Not every part is meant for you. Remember, the next audition is just around the corner.

You may have to deal with prejudice toward your choice of profession. There always seem to be kids who will tease guys for taking dance classes and being interested in the arts. I just shrug it off. If they don't get it, it's their loss.

In New York City, I like to buy tights and leotards and other dancewear at the huge Capezio dance store on Broadway. You have to wear them in dance classes, plus a nonbaggy T-shirt, so dance instructors can see how your legs are working and see your arm and shoulder positions. These are professional work clothes—but I'm sure if those teasing guys had been standing there I would have gotten razzed.

Shows and TV movies such as *High School Musical* and *Glee* have changed attitudes about guys who like singing and dancing. Still, you're going to have to be confident enough in your choices to brush off the few jokesters who will make fun of you.

My hometown friends are really supportive and come see my shows. To them, I'm just the same old Henry they grew up with, and I still go to

It's so important to have your family stay a part of your acting life. Behind us is a traveling wig shop (see how the cases fold in for shipping) on the *Beauty and the Beast* tour. My mom, dad, and sister, Charly, make my life complete.

their parties and go swimming with them when I'm home. They don't treat me any differently just because I'm onstage.

Sometimes strangers will post reviews of your work—or just random remarks about you—on internet sites. Most of the ones I've seen have been fine, but there can be some negative or crazy items posted. Don't waste your time reading them.

For me, the joy I get in being onstage outweighs any of the negatives. Nearly every day I get to learn new things about singing, acting, and dancing. I know some kids who lose their enthusiasm for the work. I don't think that will happen to me, but if it does, I know it will be the right thing to step aside. Why? Because there's no faking it under the spotlight.

12

Getting
Known in the
Business

I enjoyed talking to interviewers even at an early age. I'm 8 years old here, talking to a local TV newscaster in Washington, DC, for a segment about the history of Ford's Theatre, together with the boy who was cast as my older brother in *A Christmas Carol*. It was months before we started rehearsals and this was my first professional theater gig. I hadn't seen the script yet and hadn't even met anyone in the show!

The explosion of preteen and teen television sitcoms, kids' movies and cable shows, and televised talent competitions has ramped up interest in high school, college, and summer programs in drama, music, dance, and other performing arts.

Along with these new venues and opportunities for child performers have come new ways for your talent to be recognized. Kids are filming their own songs, monologues, dances, and comedy routines and posting them to YouTube, the video-sharing website founded in 2005, hoping to be discovered or at least generate some buzz.

Wikipedia has a list of some ninety amateur performers who have produced videos that went viral, leading some to recording contracts after they were noticed by stars such as Jay-Z, Ellen DeGeneres, and Justin Timberlake. The most famous is Justin Bieber, who was discovered on YouTube by Usher, and whose "Justin Bieber Baby" video was until very recently the most watched video in the world, with more than 500 million viewings.

Savvy high schools and summer camps are recording their annual musicals and uploading them to YouTube and social media sites. The winning monologues and scenes from high school and college drama competitions also can be seen digitally.

Like many young performers, I have my own website—check out www.henryhodges.com—and an e-mail address just for fans (henrysfans@aol.com) that is different from my personal e-mail. Casting directors frequently do Google searches of performers they are considering, looking for photographs and clips of performances that add dimension to the standard headshot and résumé.

I don't post to Twitter, but I do put up photos from my iPhone to Instagram. When I was playing Flounder in the production of *The Little Mermaid* in Sacramento, California, I posted day-to-day photos of the production on Instagram for my fans.

Make sure that anything you post is as professionally done as possible. You don't want amateur photographs or videos to detract from your nicely composed portraits and well-shot highlight reels.

Your website is an opportunity to show your range. If your amateur or professional roles all have been in dramas, your website could include some short comedy videos.

Make sure that you don't include your home address, phone number,

Some Young Performers Who Were Discovered on YouTube

It's amazing how many new talents are getting noticed online these days.

- Maria Aragon—a young Filipino-Canadian singer whose popularity soared after Lady Gaga posted a Twitter link to one of her songs

- Rebecca Black—an artist whose song "Friday" received more than 167 million viewers and many satiric imitators

- Greyson Chance—a singer discovered by Ellen DeGeneres on YouTube

- Marié Digby—a singer who posted a popular video of herself singing the Rihanna song "Umbrella"

- Jake Foushee—a young vocalist who was signed by a major arts agency after his YouTube videos garnered the notice of Ellen DeGeneres and National Public Radio

- Jamie Grace—a singer-songwriter discovered by singer TobyMac

- Alexis Jordan—a singer who was signed by Jay-Z after he watched her YouTube videos

- Charice Pempengco—a Filipina singer whose YouTube songs won her a recurring role on *Glee*

- Straight No Chaser—an Indiana University a cappella group whose "12 Days of Christmas" was a viral hit, leading Atlantic Records to sign its ten members to a five-album contract

or personal e-mail on your site, but do include the contact information for an agent or parent. You also want to check any Wikipedia entry about you to make sure it's accurate. Submit additional text, photos, and reviews that can make your entry as complete as possible.

Just as in the adult world of entertainment, there are now many state-wide and national award shows for young performers. These shows often are attended by agents and college theater program directors, and are posted online as well.

The Jimmy Awards, for example, are the National High School Musical Theater Awards. They are named for theater group owner James M. Nederlander and have been held in New York City each June since 2009. Students appear on a Broadway stage, compete for scholarships, and meet theater professionals. Broadway professionals direct young performers from stage productions in thirty states in opening and closing numbers and medleys. The awards show sells tickets to the public and also posts many of the numbers on the internet.

Nearly a dozen states host their own version of the Jimmy or Tony awards each year, drawing on the talents of the high school performers within their borders. Some cities also host annual youth-theater award shows. Pittsburgh, for example, launched the Gene Kelly Awards in 1991 to recognize high school musical theater talent.

There also are many children and youth theater conventions each year, where student performers and their advisers meet and watch excerpts from shows they might consider mounting on their school stages.

I was the celebrity guest at the Junior Theater Festival, which was held in Atlanta in 2009. At this three-day festival, there were choreography auditions, a Radio Disney dance party, and a Broadway Jr. Slam, where random casts are given an hour to rehearse a song and dance number. At the end of the festival, selected performers and technicians were chosen as All-Stars, based on their work in the prior days.

I got to see many terrific theater performances and rehearsals and participated in panel discussions. I especially enjoyed watching productions of *Beauty and the Beast Junior*, which is a shortened version performed in schools of the full-length show. I left Atlanta impressed by the energy and the sheer number of students interested in drama. You can find out more at www.itheatrics.com.

Katie Couric interviews the cast of *Chitty Chitty Bang Bang* for the *Today* show. We had to get up before dawn and get into costumes and makeup and go to Rockefeller Plaza with the full-size, and very expensive, prop car. It was quite an operation to get everyone in a show the size of *Chitty* to be ready for a song and interview in the courtyard at Rockefeller Plaza at that hour. The choreography had to be modified to fit the space and deal with the absence of the set. The orchestral music was cut to fit the time slot we were given, and prerecorded; we sang live. We were given printed "talking points" by the show's press reps, Barlow Hartman Public Relations, to help us with interview answers that would promote the show. I was picked up by a car at my apartment and taken to the NBC studios. Once we were all in costume and makeup and had had our mic check, the cast had a last meeting with Kristen Blodgette, the music director, to review some tricky changes in the song. We got the go-ahead and took our places outside on the plaza. It was "all quiet" during the commercial break. The cameras were already in place when Katie Couric came out and was handed her mic: 5,4,3,2,1—we're on! Millions of people watched the show.

Broadway on Broadway events are free concerts in Times Square that promote Broadway musicals, giving the public a peek at the songs and actors in current shows. Many fans camp out in the early hours to get spaces close to the stage and come wearing their favorite shows' T-shirts. We actors wear our show T-shirts too, rather than costumes. At the end, all the casts gather onstage to sing a final classic number, such as "Give My Regards to Broadway." They carry posters from the musicals of the season, and confetti falls from the sky and blankets all of Times Square. I love to do this gig—so long as I don't have to sweep up the confetti.

The Orphans' Home Cycle won a special Drama Desk Award, presented to the entire cast, creative team, and producers. That was one of the biggest thrills of my life. The awards are kind of a parallel to the Tony Awards, but Off-Broadway shows are eligible too. I was so proud to be part of this epic play, and so grateful to get a chance to work with its amazing director, Michael Wilson, and the irreplaceable playwright, Horton Foote.

I'm always on the lookout for new songs for my audition songbook. The Hartford, CT, library is a treasure trove, with an entire floor of nothing but sheet music. I spent hours there searching the shelves while working on *The Orphans' Home Cycle*. I also found a music book I'd never seen—the sheet music for *Chitty Chitty Bang Bang* with photos of the original Broadway cast. That's me waving in the car on the book's cover *and* in the basement of the Hartford library, making fun of myself—not for the first or last time.

Other budding performers are getting experience at workshops held by the National Storytelling Network of Jonesborough, Tennessee (www.storynet.org). Youth storytellers are part of state and national gatherings, and many of these young performers are posting their work online.

Many word slams and contests have junior divisions where young performers can get stage experience. The Moth, a New York City nonprofit that hosts storytelling events, has a website, a radio hour, and conducts performances on stages in New York City and around the country. Aspiring storytellers can pitch a story at www.themoth.org.

Teen acting academies, rock music camps, and other commercial, university, and theater-based programs cater to young would-be performers. Even if you don't go into the entertainment world, the instruction can help with your speaking and musical skills, confidence, and self-esteem. The camp staff can help record your performances and post them to your website.

Getting seen and known is a wider playing field than ever, thanks to the internet, and young performers can help their careers by building a presence on social media. But remember, keep it professional. It's very hard to erase something amateur or embarrassing from cyberspace.

It was really cool when the *Beauty and the Beast* tour landed in Washington, DC. Instead of a hotel, my mom and I got to stay in our own home. And my friends from school came to see the show—and found my name on the company performance roster inside the theater lobby.

With Christina Huschle, the last child wrangler of my career (see "A Child Wrangler Speaks," p. 148), outside the Off-Broadway Signature Theatre, where I was appearing in *The Orphans' Home Cycle*. After all the time Christina had spent "wrangling" me from one cue to the next, I'd imagine she'd have had enough of Henry Hodges! It's always flattering when fellow theatrical professionals spend their hard-earned cash to come see me in my adult roles.

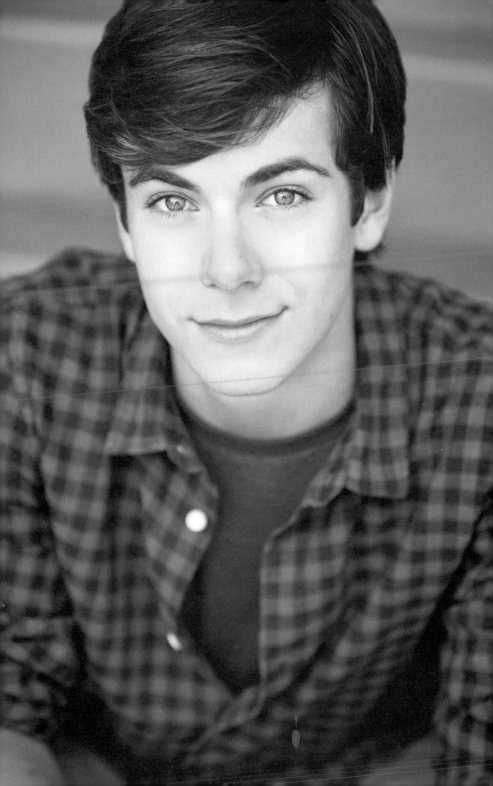

13

Transitions: Growing Up

It's important that you always actually look like your headshot. When you're still growing, that means getting a new one every year. Once you finish growing, your face continues to mature, and your headshot still has to keep pace. Here's one of my latest.

Child performers face some of their biggest challenges when they age out of kid roles. A large percentage decide they've had enough and go to rejoin their friends in high school and college. Deciding to stay in show business for a lifetime career is tricky, because the choice is not entirely yours to make.

Many child actors, singers, and dancers aren't viewed as favorably by casting directors when they go through their awkward teen years or when they try for adult roles. It's not an easy transition. The competition is harder and no one makes allowances for you because you're younger.

One of my first nonchild roles was in the *The Orphans' Home Cycle*

With Gilbert Owuor in *The Orphans' Home Cycle* at Hartford Stage, in one of my favorite scenes in the show. Gilbert, playing Leroy, a convict doing prison labor on a plantation, has just murdered another convict, and is telling me his life story. The *Cycle* demanded a big change from the kind of character arcs that end with a strong and positive feeling of closure that I was used to in musicals. It was satisfying to refine my performance night after night; every moment carried so much emotional weight. My character's story ends unresolved, and tragically: abandoned, alone, and destitute on Christmas Day. Artistically, this play is one of my proudest moments thus far.

Off-Broadway. This kind of material—serious straight theater—was really new to me, and I had to adopt a totally different acting style from the approach that had worked for me for so many years in musical theater.

The cycle comprises three evenings, each made up of three self-contained one-act plays. The story is set in Texas, from around 1900 to the beginning of the Great Depression, and concerns three generations of three families. I played the lead character, Horace Robedaux, at age fourteen. Horace is forced at age twelve to leave home, following the death of his alcoholic father, and, as you would imagine, he faces enormous hardships. The playwright, Horton Foote, tells a dark but truthful story. It's so real and so shocking that the events he describes actually occurred in the United States in that era.

When I first read the script, I didn't really get it. But once all the actors got together to read the play aloud, it came to life for me. I saw the full range of emotion Horton creates, the comedy and the tragedy. I saw a chance to prove myself.

Before I became a performer, I dodged reading and books. I would have never guessed that appearing onstage and before a camera would give me a burning interest in plays, films, and stories of all types. I'm now a dyslexic kid who enjoys reading.

To be an actor is to be a reader. One thing you learn is that theaters hire literature experts called dramaturges. They assemble huge notebooks with explanations of the background behind every line of a play. As an actor in a story, it's fun as well as work for me to read those big notebooks.

Reading the scripts and notebooks from dramaturges gets me interested in the period of history surrounding a show. Acting in *To Kill a Mockingbird* got me interested in civil rights. One night, the dramaturge arranged for the cast to come to the theater to watch a documentary on Alabama during those early years of the struggle for African American civil rights. When I was in *The Orphans' Home Cycle*, I read the autobiography of the playwright, Horton Foote. Since I was playing Horton's father as a child in the play, I was really interested in every word of that book. Reading the show's notebook helped me learn American history, especially the history of Texas at the turn of the last century.

To Kill A Mockingbird

Dramaturgy packet

Contents

Henry

Hartford Stage
January 2009
Compiled by Chris Baker

With Matthew Modine, who played
Atticus Finch in *To Kill a Mockingbird*.
Despite the heaviness of the story,
Matthew was always playful and funny
backstage, kind and generous to all the
other actors, and everyone's friend.

I like to go to the library at Lincoln Center in New York and watch classic performances in older musicals and plays that it has on tape. There are also many great classic films to learn about and see. In the summer, my family and I go to the free Monday night outdoor films in Bryant Park in New York City, just behind the main branch of the public library.

Once I hit my teen years, things on- and offstage changed. Legally, producers were still obliged to provide me with a child wrangler, but I no longer followed her around and she no longer reminded me which wing to enter from. In professional theater, after age sixteen you are in an adult business without an adult looking over your shoulder.

Everyone's expectations of you are higher once you're older. Skills that were novel for a child actor are routine for young adult actors. During auditions, everyone has advanced skills, in singing, in hip-hop, in gymnastics. They've really honed their craft. The competition is generally more consistent. All the performers without advanced skills have been weeded out. But the biggest change is the emotional maturity that's expected.

Here's an example of the kind of child behavior that's no longer acceptable once you become a teenager. During *Mary Poppins*, one child actor said he was not feeling well and he was thinking about not going on. The stage manager, assistant director, and director were called. The child first told them he felt "fifty-fifty" about going onstage, then remembered he had relatives coming to the show, and said maybe he would take the stage.

This annoyed the directors because the entire cast's attitude should be to give a great show no matter who is in the seats. The child wanted the adults to beg him to go on, but instead they just instantly replaced him for that show. His attempt looked to me like a plea for attention that backfired. In the second act, he made a halfhearted comment that he was ready to go on now. Of course, that didn't happen. His mother gave him so much heat for it later, but the damage was done. He was never considered totally dependable after that. His behavior didn't cost him the job, but it changed stage management's outlook on him. If he had been a late teen or young adult actor, his reliability would have been seriously questioned (though according to Equity rules I don't think anyone could be fired for what he did).

Once you hit your teen years, you are competing with actors at a wide range of ages for parts. It can be hard for a teenager to get a teenage

A Talent Agent Speaks

 Steve Maihack is my agent at the Stewart Talent Agency in New York City. This boutique agency also has offices in Chicago and Atlanta and represents stage and film actors, directors, musical artists, voice-over talent, on-camera commercial actors, speakers, and new-media talent.

Q: *Why do relatively few child actors make a successful transition to young-adult and adult roles?*

A: A child actor starts at an age when acting is fun, it's role-playing and part of natural childhood development. The ones who are really good treat acting like playing a sport. When she or he gets older, a child branches out and the interest level can diminish. The ones who make it have wanted to perform for their entire lives.

Q: *How can a child actor improve those odds? What skills and attitudes do you find necessary?*

A: Part of it is being prepared for everything. Being off book for auditions and really doing your research. There's an independence factor that comes into play with more successful child actors. Those who are slightly more independent of their family have a better shot.

Q: *As an agent, you are besieged by hopeful performers looking for a way in. What is your advice to them?*

A: You have to realize pretty quickly what the child wants to do. A lot of parents see kids on TV and film and think their own kids would be great. You don't want child actors to grow up and feel they were forced into it by their families.

Q: *How do you handle young teens who have had success as children but are having difficulty getting roles? Is it ever wise to take a break for several years until they can start auditioning for adult roles?*

A: It does help to take a break to help find out who they are as young adults. We see kids taking breaks at the end of elementary school or junior high. Or starting again after college. They gain their own opinions about life and that helps.

Q: *Does the rise of e-mailed auditions mean that young performers no longer need to travel to New York and Los Angeles for work?*

A: With technology you really don't have to fly or go anywhere for auditions. Everything is a point or a click away. That's if the casting office will take tapes, and most do.

Q: *Why has Henry been able to make the leap from Disney musicals to straight plays?*

A: We saw in Henry early on that he is on a journey with his career. He was lucky to be the lead in multiple Disney productions. He's learned how to develop a taste for drama, plays. He studied to get onto the adult path.

Doing the voice-over work for the animated film *Snow Buddies*. To give the sound engineers maximum control over the recorded material, each voice actor is usually isolated from the others. Sometimes you don't even read with the other actors in your scenes. Even though there were four other actors playing my brother and sister dogs in *Snow Buddies* and *Space Buddies*, I only ever met one of them, because the rest recorded in LA and I was in New York.

part. Producers often use older actors to avoid the expenses of hiring teachers and child wranglers.

The casting breakdown for the part of Flounder in *The Little Mermaid* specified an eighteen- to twenty-two-year-old boy who could play a believable sixteen-year-old. So, okay, I got the job. The breakdown for his friend Ariel specified a believable eighteen-year-old. I was looking forward to meeting the girl who would play my best friend. She turned out to be the awesome and beautiful Jessica Grové, who was thirty years old, married, and had a baby! No one in the cast was even close to my age.

Another difference between acting as a kid and as a young adult is that young adult actors may cultivate long-lasting professional relationships with casting directors and producers. Those friendships can (though not often) affect who gets chosen for parts. In one show I tried out for, several of the teen actors' parents were investors in the show.

For me, stepping over the age barrier was both challenging and fun. Right now, I'm living and auditioning in New York, but I also have stayed in Los Angeles for several months to audition for television shows and films there.

I took classes for one year at a community college in my home county in Maryland, but I found that my focus was split if I tried to combine acting with schoolwork. So I'm no longer taking college classes, but I am going on auditions as often as I can.

I'm continuing to hone my craft by continuing to vocalize, keeping myself in shape, and reading scripts. My talent agency in New York continues to look for roles for me. After I performed in *The Little Mermaid* in Sacramento, I was asked to do a reading of the show for the original team that created *The Little Mermaid* on Broadway. At that reading, songwriter Alan Menken actually played the role of the chef, singing the part he wrote. Hearing him in that part—that was an experience!

The talent world is different in California. Everyone, from the casting directors to the agents, expresses more enthusiasm about you, but that positive energy doesn't translate into more roles. It just represents that general Los Angeles feeling—everyone is "wonderful" or "terrific."

I have frequently made it to callbacks, sometimes to repeated callbacks, but then my Los Angeles manager would be told that the show or film was "going in a different direction." When you get general feedback

My road to *The Little Mermaid* was a long one. I auditioned for the original Broadway cast, but was already in *Mary Poppins* at the time. During the first auditions for *Mermaid*, there was talk of Flounder riding a waveboard, but in the end he wore sneakers with built-in wheels in the heels instead. Years later, the show was reimagined and I was thrilled to learn that Flounder had been changed from a 9-year-old to a teenager. As a professional actor at any age, you basically only get cast in parts appropriate to your looks (which means, to some degree, characters close to your real age). It isn't like being in school shows, where you can be cast as Tevye, the father in *Fiddler on the Roof*, when you are only 15. When I auditioned for the part of Flounder, I rode my own waveboard into the audition room. After I was cast, the waveboard was incorporated into the show. My first entrance took me perilously close to the orchestra pit every night—but I never fell in.

like that, you question what you could have done better in the auditions. Even if they tell you the role went to someone older or taller, it's just as possible that you weren't good enough. You replay things in your head, wondering how you could have made a better impression or come across stronger.

But you can't overthink such setbacks; you have to prepare for the next audition. Basically, my motto with each audition is YOU'RE GETTING CLOSER TO THE JOB YOU'RE GOING TO GET. I'm busy, so I don't mope around if I don't get a part. But it's only natural to be disappointed. When you've gotten a lot of callbacks, and you've gotten to a chemistry read (where you and another actor who has already been cast are put together to see how that pairing works), it doesn't feel great when the role doesn't come your way.

I put a lot of effort into auditions, but you just have to roll with the punches. If you get into a negative mindset, you'll go to the next audition in a poor frame of mind, thinking, *I'm not going to get it*. What I tell myself is *I can do this. I can get this job. Why not me?*

As a young adult, casting directors and your managers and agents want you to have the confidence and skills you need to express many emotions on all sorts of levels. You aren't just a kid anymore. No allowances will be made for you. They have to see what you can do. They are not going to try to pull it out of you.

Acting as a young adult remains a big commitment for most young actors' families. You typically don't make enough money to live on your own, so you are dependent on your parents for housing. It's the lucky few who can deal with renting an apartment in New York and whose family can handle the logistics of devoting so much focus to one child. It's helped me enormously that we moved to New York several years ago and live in the Theater District, and that I was homeschooled.

My dreams for my future include playing some of the classic musical theater roles, like the Phantom in *Phantom of the Opera* and the master of ceremonies in *Cabaret*. I'd love to sing Sondheim. I'd love to act in more classic theater, including Shakespeare. I think I could do Puck, and Ariel. I also want to work on feature films. I'd love a part like the one a young Leonardo DiCaprio played in *What's Eating Gilbert Grape?* or a challenging role like Dustin Hoffman's in *Rain Man*. Both comedy and drama appeal to me for television, particularly an edgy show like *Dexter*. I would act in anything with Anthony Hopkins!

I'd also love to teach and maybe direct. I've coached some children in parts and seen them get cast in Broadway shows. That's a thrill. I know that my future always will include performing. I have to say it's in my blood.

A view of the stage for *The Orphans' Home Cycle* at Hartford Stage, set for act 3 of part 1. The technician is running a "dimmer check": Before every show, the lighting crew has to make sure that every theatrical light is working correctly and is correctly focused. It's calm onstage, but backstage is very busy—organized chaos—as the actors get into their makeup and costumes.

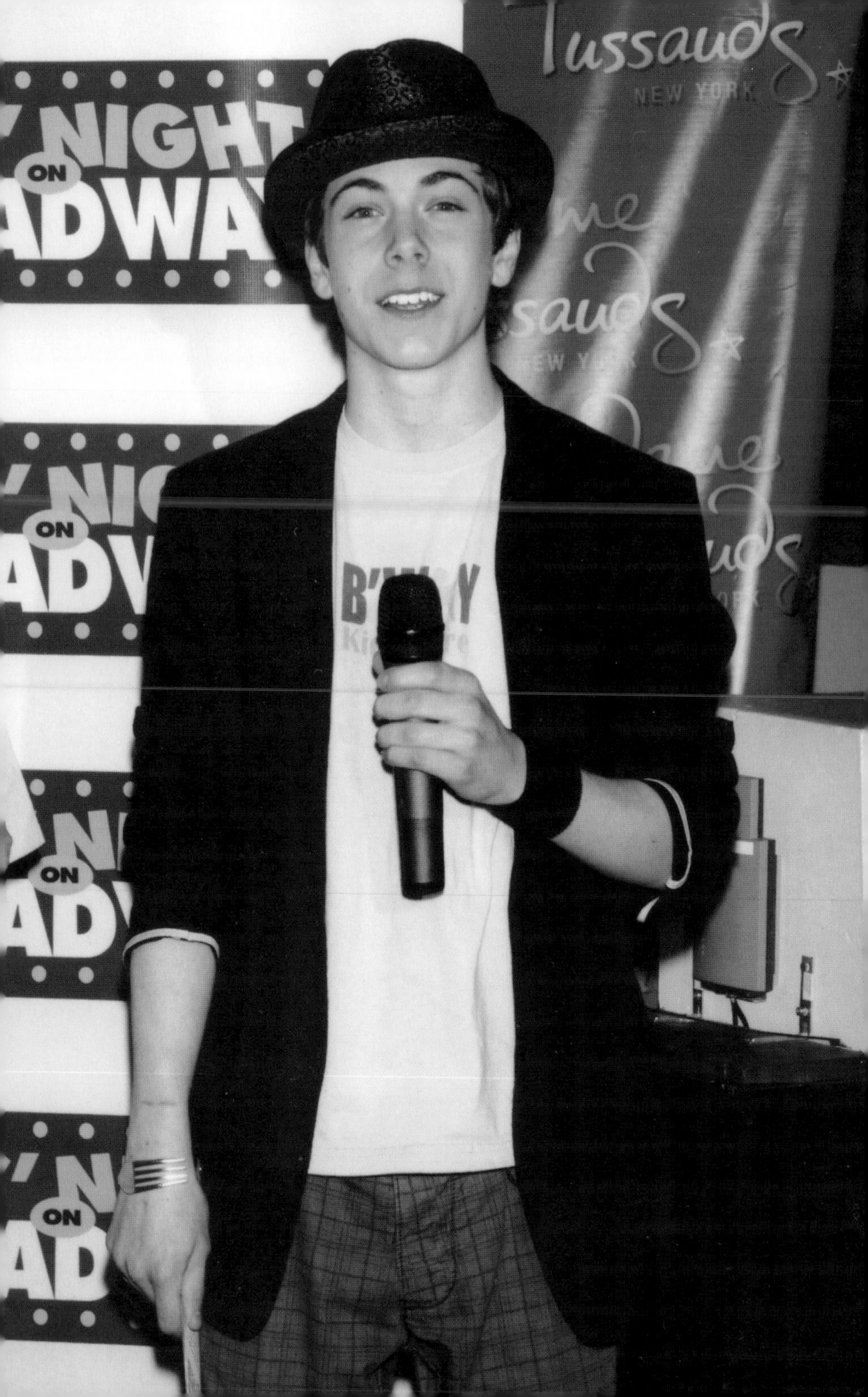

NIGHT
ON
Tussauds
NEW YORK

14

Giving Back, Moving Forward

Kids' Night on Broadway lets young fans see a Broadway show for free. Here I'm introducing *High School Musical* star Corbin Bleu at Madame Tussauds wax museum, and encouraging parents to bring their children to these free performances. Kids' Night takes place every February and now includes Broadway shows that are traveling throughout the U.S. It's one way the theater community is trying to "grow" the next generation of theatergoers.

Performers are not only artists and entertainers. We are citizens too. And growing up in public gives you obligations to your community that go beyond the work you do to get a show onstage. For me it has always gone without saying that I'd contribute in any way I could to my show's success, including participating in the fund-raising activities that are often built around individual shows. I've signed five hundred or a thousand posters at a time that were sold or auctioned to raise money for charities, until my fingers could no longer hold a Sharpie pen, but I was always glad to do it. I've sung on CDs recorded as fund-raisers too. It always seems to me to demand minimum effort for maximum return, especially compared to what some of the people who are helped by these charities have to go through. Not every actor says yes to these events, but I always volunteer. For a performer, the only difference between a regular show and a charity fund-raising event is that you perform for free. But it's still a show: a chance to meet new people, to learn new things, to interact with colleagues and with an audience. Always say yes!

One of the most important theater charities is Broadway Cares/Equity Fights AIDS, which pays for health clinics, food service and meal delivery, housing, and emergency assistance programs for theater people living with HIV/AIDS across the country. You've probably seen actors holding baskets after certain performances, collecting money at the exits. The dollars we collect for Broadway Cares also fund six programs of the Actors Fund, including the Phyllis Newman Women's Health Initiative and the Al Hirschfeld Free Health Clinic. (Phyllis Newman is a stage actress and Al Hirschfeld was a famous theater cartoonist.)

Another group is the Broadway Green Alliance, which has "green captains" in most theaters who work on recycling efforts, such as reusing binders for scripts, and promote the use of stainless steel water bottles and lower-energy lightbulbs. The alliance participates in Kids' Night on Broadway, which is usually a week in February when kids ages six to eighteen can see Broadway shows free with a paying adult. Several Times Square restaurants let kids eat free during that week too. Other cities around the country have their versions of Kids' Night and it's a great way to see a show at no cost.

One of my friends, the Broadway producer Kelly Gonda, founded a kids-only service group, Broadway Kids Care. Many child actors came

Giving Back

Kelly Gonda, a former child actress, explains why she started Broadway Kids Care, which is open to current and former child actors interested in community service.

Q: *What motivated you to bring child performers into charitable work?*

A: I saw that children could do more and wanted to do more. It helps the children know they have value and worth even when they aren't in a show.

Q: *What projects has Broadway Kids Care undertaken?*

A: We raised money for UNICEF and participated in Oprah Winfrey's global initiative on [supplying] diapers. We went to the Actors Fund home in New Jersey and sang and learned their stories. We stuffed Easter baskets for Freedom House, a New York emergency shelter for disabled victims of domestic violence and their families run by Barrier Free Living. We'd gather the kids between their shows on Wednesdays and work on knitting scarves for our soldiers and for the homeless.

Q: *How did the children respond?*

A: It was so beneficial to them. At 7:30 p.m., they are putting pancake makeup on, but by 10:00 p.m., they are human beings who hit the pavement. They worked with Vanessa Brown, one of the terrific child guardians [wranglers], who are some of the unsung heroes on Broadway, along with the carpenters and ushers. This work kept the kids humble.

Q: *In addition to good deeds, what other benefits did this charitable effort bring?*

A: At the end of the day, the children looked in the mirror and were proud of themselves. They liked the reflection.

It's not just adult performers who give back. Broadway Kids Care does a lot of community-service projects. That's me in the back row, with a backwards ball cap, beside founder Kelly Gonda, as child performers put on chef's hats and aprons to run a bake sale.

together to hold bake sales, make crafts, and help raise money for international children's charities. Every Wednesday we'd gather between our matinee and the evening show for a pizza dinner and work on our charity projects. I really loved giving back with that group.

Recently, the Broadway Kids Care performers sang at the annual lighting of the UNICEF snowflake. That's a huge outdoor Christmas ornament at Fifty-Seventh Street and Fifth Avenue that is lit to mark the beginning of the holiday gift-giving season around the world.

I feel very fortunate that I've had the opportunity to work with the best of the best, with performers of limitless talent, people who have always been a hundred percent supportive of me in what I was doing and wanted to accomplish. For me, the best thing about working in the

The stage door of the Lunt-Fontanne Theatre.

Gifts from family, friends, fellow cast members, and crew, on opening night of *Chitty Chitty Bang Bang.*

theater, the thing I love the most, is rehearsing, creating the show, working together with actors and singers and dancers I can look up to, admire, learn from, and emulate. Having my family and my colleagues behind me has enabled me always to look toward the future with hope. I've known other performers who didn't have some of the support that I've had. Some of them have made it, and some of them have not.

I really have been so lucky. I've never yet had to have a support job, never had to show up at auditions half dead from waiting tables till all hours. I've never had to share a tiny New York apartment with five other struggling actors. I've never had to audition at open calls—which aren't known as "cattle calls" for nothing. Even though I always feel that I could have done better in everything, that none of my work has ever been perfect, I feel fortunate that I can look back on the things that I've done and be proud of what I have accomplished.

I wrote this book to help other young, aspiring performers, to give you the practical information that I wish—and my mom wishes too!—that we had had when I was starting out. Once upon a time I was just a frustrated undersize dyslexic kid who felt he had no place to be—my school just had no room for me. In the theater, I felt immediately that I belonged. I felt included, accepted, allowed to grow into who I really am and am meant to be. I didn't have to change; I only had to become myself. I believe that if you are meant to be onstage, one way or the other, you will be. I encourage everyone to try.

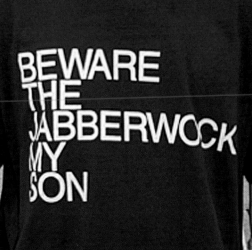

Sources of Help

Young performers often don't realize just how many resources there are out there to help you get started and build your career. Here are some of the best sources of information on working in theater, film, and television.

Specialty Newspapers/Magazines/Reports

- *Back Stage* A weekly tabloid trade journal that is a popular source for audition notices. Single issues: $2.95; subscriptions: $99 per year. Published by Prometheus Global Media, 770 Broadway, New York, NY 10003; www.backstage.com.
- *Call Sheet Back Stage* Formerly the *Ross Reports Television & Film*, this bimonthly directory lists New York City and Los Angeles agents who are franchised by one or more of the major talent unions, including SAG (the Screen Actors Guild), which has merged with AFTRA (the American Federation of Television and Radio Artists), and AEA (Actors' Equity Association). Published by Prometheus Global Media, 770 Broadway, New York, NY 10003. Single issues: $9.95; subscriptions: $60 per year. Subscribers may search for agents and casting directors on the publication's website: www.backstage.com.
- *Variety* A weekly magazine covering film, TV, and theater that began in 1905, covering vaudeville. Features industry news, reviews, and box office grosses. Available at newsstands and by online subscription at www.variety.com. Students receive a discount.
- *Theatrical Index* A weekly trade publication about Broadway, Off-Broadway, touring shows, and many regional theaters. Subscriptions cost $425 per year, and include access to its subscription-only site, www.theatricalindex.com.

Advice Books

- *Raising a Star: The Parents' Guide to Helping Kids Break into Theater, Film, Television, or Music,* by Nancy Carson, with Jacqueline Shannon (New York: St. Martin's Griffin, 2005).
- *Your Child in Film and Television,* by Allison Cohee (Mumbai: Jaico, 2006). Especially strong on film and extra roles, with sample contracts, payroll vouchers, and commercial engagement contracts.
- *Admit One: Ten Steps to Choosing Your Acting or Musical Theatre College Program,* by Chelsea Cipolla and John West (New York: My College Audition, 2011). A student guide to choosing among college acting and musical theater programs.
- *An Actor's Guide: Your First Year in Hollywood,* by Michael Nicholas (New York: Allworth Press, 2010). Focuses on places to live, first jobs, how to build credits, and where to get training.
- *Ask an Agent: Everything Actors Need to Know About Agents,* by Margaret Emory (New York: Backstage Books, 2005). The author writes the *Ask an Agent* column in *Back Stage* magazine.
- *Voice-Over Voice Actor: What It's Like Behind the Mic,* by Yuri Lowenthal and Tara Platt (Hollywood, CA: Bug Bot Press, 2009). A detailed look at voice-over work and contracts.

Where to Find Scripts and Books

- **The Drama Book Shop** 250 W. 40th St., New York, NY 10018; 212-944-0595; toll-free U.S. and Canada: 800-322-0595; fax 212-730-8739; www.dramabookshop.com. In New York's Theater District since 1917.
- **Samuel French** www.samuelfrench.com; with branches in New York City, Hollywood, and London. French's catalog of some 7,000 play scripts may be accessed online, and you can listen to clips from musicals on the company's website.

Where to Find Theatrical Sheet Music and CDs

- **Dowling Music** 109 W. 57th St., 2nd floor, New York, NY 10019; 212-799-8059, toll-free 800-952-7526; www.dowlingmusic.com. Dowling stocks sheet music from Broadway to opera inside historic Steinway

Hall, built in 1925. Texas branch: 2615 Southwest Freeway, #220, Houston, TX 77098; 713-529-2676. A reliable source for all kinds of sheet music in Houston, since 1943.

- **The Juilliard Store** 44 W. 66th St., New York, NY 10023; 212-799-5000 ext. 237; store@juilliard.edu. More than 90,000 CDs, DVDs, MP3s, and sheet music are available in the newly renovated store that serves The Juilliard School, one of the nation's leading conservatories of dance, drama, and music.

Where to View Filmed Plays and TV Shows

- **Theatre on Film and Tape Archive (TOFT)** 40 Lincoln Center Plaza, New York, NY 10023; appointment line: 212-870-1642; online catalog at www.nypl.org/research/lpa. Open Mon. noon–8:00 p.m.; Tues.– Sat. noon–6:00 p.m. Part of the New York Public Library for the Performing Arts. More than 5,000 tapes of stage shows from 1970 on can be viewed in the Lucille Lortel Room in Lincoln Center.
- **The Paley Center for Media** New York branch: 25 W. 52nd St., New York, NY 10019; 212-621-6800. Los Angeles branch: 465 N. Beverly Dr., Beverly Hills, CA 90210; 310-786-1091. Both branches: www.paleycenter.org. Both branches of this archive house radio programs from the 1920s on and television programs from the 1940s on. The centers feature screening rooms, industry seminars, and online synopses of the programs in the collection. Admission is $10 for adults, $8 for students, and $5 for children under 14.

Online Resources for Performers

- **www.actorsequity.org** Details on how to join the union repre-senting actors and stage managers in the U.S., as well as student outreach programs and free members' workshops.
- **www.sagaftra.org** The home of the Screen Actors Guild–American Federation of Television and Radio Artists, including these subsites: **youngperformers.sag.org** has a handbook for young performers that is free to download; **www.sagfoundation.org** offers informa-tion on industry seminars and access to the Screen Actors Guild voice-over studio and training (free to members).

- **www.mybroadwaydreams.com** The not-for-profit Broadway Dreams Foundation offers a performing arts training program comprising master classes, Triple Threat workshops (acting, singing, and dance), songwriting classes, and mock auditions, all taught by Broadway actors, casting directors, agents, and choreographers. BDF is linked with theaters in communities across the country, including Atlanta, Los Angeles, Philadelphia, Chicago, Omaha, Dallas, Connecticut, and South Carolina. BDF's year-round classes and summer workshops have a fee, but scholarships are available. The mission is to serve all, regardless of ability to pay. Students range from ages 7 to 65. Benefit showcase performances are held before paying audiences.
- **www.bizparentz.org** Information on laws, scams, and how-to's for families of children working in the entertainment industry. Includes a page on how to find legitimate Disney auditions.
- **www.nacacnet.org** Listings of the spring and fall Performing and Visual Arts College Fairs held in some twenty cities nationwide by the National Association for College Admissions Counseling. Some eighty college performing arts programs and conservatories participate.
- **www.schoolsfortheatre.com** Searchable guide to colleges offering theater arts programs, from acting to drama therapy. Offers direct links to colleges' audition requirements pages.
- **www.edta.org** Site for *Dramatics* magazine, aimed at the high school drama field.
- **www.castingabout.com** A $10-per-month service run by *Back Stage* describing what shows casting agents are handling.
- **www.theatricalindex.com** A subscription-only site ($19.95 per month) for weekly information on shows on Broadway, Off-Broadway, touring productions, and regional theaters.
- **www.backstage.com/prodny** Listing of current New York film and TV productions.
- **www.backstage.com/prodla** Listing of current Los Angeles film and TV productions.
- **www.backstage.com/unions-guilds** Listing of theatrical unions, guilds, and associations.
- **www.backstage.com/cdlabels** Listing in mailing-labels format of talent agents, casting directors, and personal managers in New York

and Los Angeles; available for $19.50 per list.

- **www.playbill.com** News about Broadway, Off-Broadway, regional, and London theaters, plus discount ticket offers.
- **www.hollywoodreporter.com** Film and TV news from the website of the weekly paid magazine *Hollywood Reporter*. Includes guides to TV pilots and box office reports.
- **www.broadwayworld.com** News about all levels of theater, including Equity and non-Equity auditions, a high school theater center, and BWW Junior, which reviews children's theater and movie offerings. Publishes yearly directories of upcoming show listings for thousands of colleges and high schools, with cast lists and videos.
- **www.theatermania.com** Interviews, videos, reviews, and discount tickets.
- **www.breaking-character.com** Theater news, including festivals and high school and college plays, created by Samuel French, the nation's oldest publisher of plays.
- **www.allmusicindustrycontacts.com** A subscription-only site listing producers, arrangers, and other musical talent.
- **www.sidesexpress.com** A subscription-only service that makes sides and scripts available from agents in electronic form.

Other Sources

Your state's film and television commission may offer information on extras or background casting for films and TV shows being produced in state.

Words to Know

The theater has its own language, including many terms unfamiliar to outsiders and familiar words used in special ways. Here are some of the most important words to know.

Blocking The process of figuring out actors' positions and movement from place to place onstage, from each entrance to the following exit, led by the director and/or choreographer and their assistants. Performers also use the word *blocking* to refer to the onstage movement itself once it is set and memorized.

Breakdown A synopsis of a theater or film project that describes each character, usually by the age, height, and look sought, sent to agents by casting directors. Also known as *call-outs*.

Call time The time you are called to be present and ready to work in the theater or on a movie set.

Cheating Turning partially toward (cheating in) or away from (cheating out) the audience while remaining engaged with other actors onstage. This lets the audience see your face while maintaining the illusion that you are facing your scene partners.

Cold read An audition or rehearsal during which you read the script for the first time.

Cue lights Backstage electric lights that the stage manager flashes to give silent cues to actors, telling them when to enter onstage. The *standby* signal is usually a flashing red or yellow. The *go* signal is typically a steady green.

Cue-to-cue An onstage rehearsal that skips almost all the actors' lines and jumps from one technical cue to the next. The purpose of the cue-to-cue is to make sure that the placement and duration of all the cues for lighting, sound, and movement of scenic elements are correct. In

musicals, the cue-to-cue may require the performers to sing the beginning and end of every song; likewise for dance numbers. Cue-to-cues
can feel very jumpy and awkward and be very tiring for the performers, but they are very important.

Dramaturge (or dramaturg) A literary expert hired by a theater either
to shape a script or to provide research to the cast on a play's
background.

Dry tech A rehearsal in the theater with all the stage crew but without
the performers that allows the crew to rehearse all their cues.

Equity The nickname for Actors' Equity, the union representing some
49,000 actors and stage managers in the U.S. Some auditions are open
only to Equity members.

Ghost light A bulb mounted on a stand that illuminates the stage so that
the crew can find their way when they enter the building and the last
people departing the stage can see the exits. The ghost light burns
when the stage is empty, preventing the theater from going dark.

Greenroom The lounge in a theater where performers hang out when
they are not onstage or the television studio lounge where performers
(or guests on talk shows, etc.) wait before going on camera.

"House open" The words the stage manager broadcasts backstage to the
company and crew when the doors open to let the audience enter the
theater.

Industrial A film or live show done for a corporation.

LORT theaters The League of Resident Theaters, an association of
seventy-six regional theaters, arranged in four tiers labeled A to D,
depending on their box office receipts. More Equity actors work in
LORT theaters than on Broadway or in touring shows.

Marks Spots on the stage where performers stand and where props and
set pieces are placed; also marks on the stage that performers use to
orient themselves in space. Marks are often indicated with colored
tape, glow-in-the-dark tape, or numbers.

Off book When you have memorized the script and are working
without it.

Proscenium The arch separating the stage from the auditorium; from the
Ancient Greek word *proskēnion,* meaning "in front of the stage."

Raked stage A stage that slopes upward away from the audience. A
raked stage allows the audience to see the performers better than a

flat stage in many theaters, especially if the audience seating area is not raked. Sometimes the stage itself is flat, but the set built on it is raked. Raked stages can be very difficult to dance on—especially for turns and jumps!

Reel or **demo tape** A CD or e-mailed file with a sampling of your best work, usually one to five minutes long.

SAG The Screen Actors Guild, a film union now merged with the American Federation of TV and Radio Artists: the union for actors, dancers, singers, voice-over artists, etc. Features an actor online casting service for members.

Sides Pages of a script supplied to actors before an audition.

Slating Announcing your name and agent before you begin an on-camera audition. Slating helps the casting director remember the actors who audition. (The term comes from the little chalkboard slates with a clapper used in shooting movies to note the scene and take number before each shot.)

Speed-through A rehearsal during which the performers work on lines, without doing the blocking and other movement. Actors can also "speed through" their blocking quickly without saying their lines. And dancers can speed through a number by marking (indicating) the movement quickly, without the music, usually to make sure that the spacing has been worked out correctly—so no one will bump into or trip over anyone else!

Strike After the last performance, when the set is dismantled and costumes, props, and lighting equipment are put away.

Supernumeraries People hired to play small nonsinging parts in operas (and nondancing parts in story ballets such as *Swan Lake*). Supernumeraries often appear in crowd scenes. From the Latin word *supernumerarius*, meaning a soldier added to a legion after it is complete.

Thrust stage A stage, part of which extends into the audience, with the viewers typically seated on three sides.

Vom An entrance/exit to the stage through the house, where the audience is seated. From *vomitorium*, an entrance/exit passage in an ancient Roman theater or amphitheater.

Wrangler The adult who supervises child performers backstage during breaks and while traveling for touring shows.

Acknowledgments

I would like to thank Thomas Schumacher and Ridley Pearson for their encouragement; Wendy Lefkon, editorial director of Disney Editions, for making this book possible; all the people at Disney Publishing who have helped to make the book a reality, including managing editor Jennifer Eastwood and Wendy's assistant, editor Jessica Ward; Warren Meislin, who patiently and expertly proofread these pages twice; and those responsible for making these pages beautiful, designer Clark Wakabayashi and his team at Welcome Books, and compositor Susan Gerber at R&S Book Composition.

When we started to work on the manuscript, I had no idea what it takes to make a book, and how many stages there are in the process. Now I know why authors thank their editors! This goes double for our editor, Christopher Caines, who is organized, smart, and funny, and who never lost his patience with my constant misspellings and jumbled numbers. Christopher, I can't thank you enough.

My gratitude goes to these people and organizations in the business who have taken the time and interest to help me become a better performer: Devon Abner, David Austin, Joe Baker, Dusty Bennett, Charlie Boyer, Marlene Brooker, Ashley Brown, Vanessa Brown, Danny Burstein, Camera Ready Kids, Carleigh Cappetta Schultz, Carson Adler Agency, Glenn Casale, CESD Talent, Murphy Cross, Steven Cirillo, Chris Curtis, Jim DeMarse, Christopher Dykton, Raúl Esparza, Scott Evans, Sir Richard Eyre, Hallie Foote, Ryan Gielen, Kelly and Lou Gonda, Dominique Hogue, James Houghton, Daniel Jenkins, Jay Johnson, Paul Kreppel, Linda Lenzi, Rebecca Luker, Anthony Lyn, Diane McFarland, Gary C. Mead, Matthew Modine, Kenny Ortega, Robert and Robbie Sherman, Stewart Talent, Sweeney Entertainment, Max Williams, Bobby Wilson, Kathleen Wilson, and Michael Wilson.

Grateful thanks to my friends who have stuck with me through it all: Annette and David Abrams; Maya and Shayna Berman; Alex and Zach Burstein; Kimberly Cappetta; Christopher and Ryan Cree; Wilma Drake; the Pittsburgh Funts; Katie, Lizzie, and Patrick Henney; Jojo Lenzi; Jackson Warner Lewis; Chris Matos; the Abilene Pughs; Hannah Sangillo; Isabel Soufront; Keegan Sullivan; Steve Webber; and Jack Williams.

And, of course, many thanks to Peggy Engel for her friendship, expert advice, and encouragement.

H.H.
New York City
November 2012

Henry and I would like to thank the theatrical professionals who so generously donated their time and expertise to the interviews and background research for this book, for their diverse perspectives on the lives of young performers: Jim Carnahan, Amelia DeMayo, Kelly Gonda, Ray Hesselink, Anne Marie Hurlbut, Christina Huschle, Jennifer Crier Johnston, Yuka Kawazu, Muriel Kester, Michael Lavine, Steven Maihack, Jennifer Maloney, Alex Molinari, Janine Molinari, and Alan Simon.

I also thank Broadway directors David Esbjornson and Michael Mayer and actress Nora Kirkpatrick for their invaluable discussions about the worlds of stage and screen.

Special appreciation, always, to my twin sister, Allison Engel, for her help with this book, and to my husband, Bruce Adams, for his patience, and to our own star performers, Emily Adams and Hugh Adams.

My ultimate thanks to fellow Edgemorons, Henry and Jane Hodges, for their varied experiences, specific advice, and endearing recollections.

M.E.
Bethesda, MD
November 2012

Illustrations Credits

The authors gratefully acknowledge the following for their kind permission to reproduce the images and ephemera in this book:

Marlene Brooker/Marlene's Fantastic Foto Favors: 8, 184
Courtesy of Jim Carnahan: 78
Michael Carroll: vi, 37, 64, 87, 89, 155
Courtesy of Disney Theatrical Group: 77, 80, 84, 122, 131, 144
T. Charles Erickson, Hartford Stage: 96, 99, 100, 140, 190, 192, 199, 206
Courtesy of Kelly Gonda: 203
Courtesy of Ray Hesselink: 36
Henry Hodges: 28, 153
Jane Hodges: xv, xvi, 4, 5, 7, 8, 11, 12, 14, 15, 16, 17, 18, 19, 20, 21, 23, 24, 26, 30, 31, 38, 56, 71, 76, 86, 89, 91, 94, 103, 112, 115, 118, 119, 121, 124, 132, 137, 141, 142, 143, 146, 157, 158, 161, 162, 167, 170, 175, 178, 183, 185, 187, 195, 200, 204, 205, 207, 214, 218
James Hodges: 35
Courtesy of Christina Huschle: 148
Courtesy of Jennifer Crier Johnston: 126
Glenn Jussen/Jussen Studio: 3
Courtesy of Muriel Kester: 114
Courtesy of Michael Lavine: 68
Linda Lenzi, Broadway World: 16, 18, 184, 208
Courtesy of Steve Maihack: 194
Courtesy of Jennifer Maloney: 60
Joan Marcus: viii, x
Walter McBride Photography: 6
Courtesy of Alex Molinari: 40
Courtesy of Janine Molinari: 32
Carol Pratt/Carol Pratt Photography: 129
Tom Radcliffe: xii, 44, 46
Vince Trupsin: 188
José Luis Villegas: 5, 48, 52, 53, 58, 59, 90, 105, 169, 197, 222